LITTLE MOMENTS

WENDY CLAIRE MANGEANT

little moments

*true short stories,
big life lessons*

COPYRIGHT © 2024 WENDY CLAIRE MANGEANT
All rights reserved.

LITTLE MOMENTS
True Short Stories, Big Life Lessons

FIRST EDITION

ISBN   978-1-5445-4677-3   *Paperback*
         978-1-5445-4678-0   *Ebook*

To You

From Me

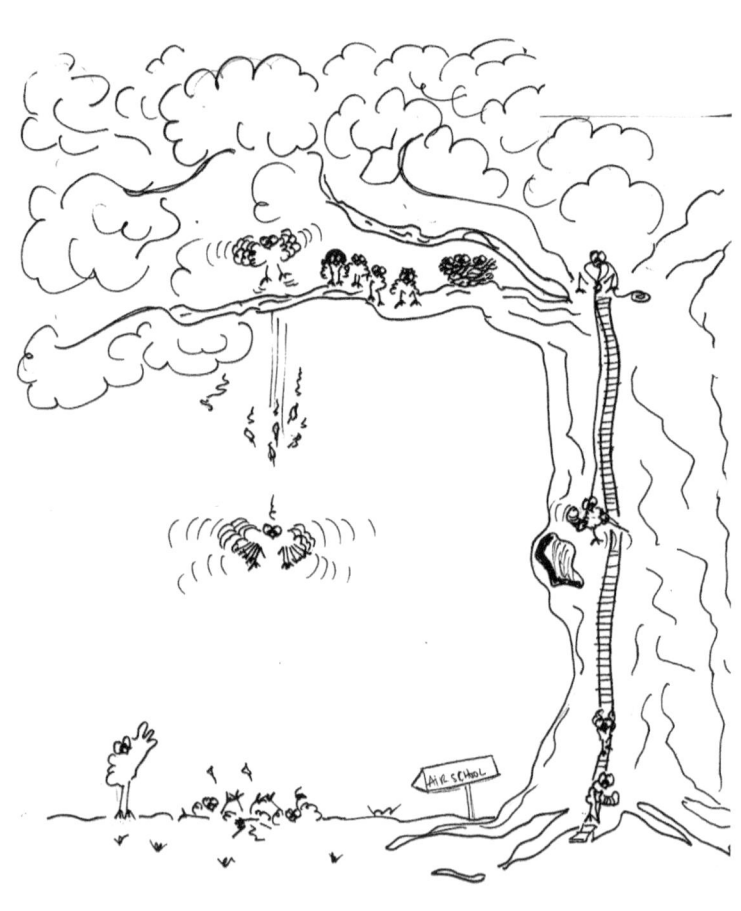

10 Life Skills for Well-Being

#1. Holding the Peace

#2. Believing in the Process

#3. Offering Feelings

#4. Letting Go

#5. Being Loving & Respectful

#6. Looking for the Big Picture

#7. Watching Which Way We're Going

#8. Listening Within

#9. Taking One Step at a Time

#10. Being Positive

Contents

A VERY SHORT INTRO 13

LIFE SKILL: #1. HOLDING THE PEACE

1. HOLD THE PEACE 17
2. PAT-PAT 21
3. ALL TUCKED IN 23
4. WHERE WOULD I BE IF I WERE A PASSPORT? 25
5. THE FLAMING SWORD 29
6. SQUISH, SQUISH 31
7. WHOOSH! 35
8. ALWAYS THE SKY 39

LIFE SKILL: #2. BELIEVING IN THE PROCESS

9. THUMP-THUMP 43
10. POTATOES WITH PA 47
11. F-R-E-D 51
12. NOT READY YET 55
13. PAR LAY VOO FRAN SAY? 59
14. MY HAPPY LIST 63
15. BRIGHTER IN THE MORNING 67
16. EVERY HUNDRED YEARS 71

LIFE SKILL: #3. OFFERING FEELINGS

17. OFFERING FEELINGS 77
18. WE DON'T BITE 79
19. FUZZY TEETH 83
20. LITTLE KINDNESSES 87
21. KNOCK-KNOCK 89
22. WAIT THREE DAYS 93
23. TALKING LIKE A TENNIS BALL 97
24. SITTING SMALLER THAN SUNFLOWERS 101

LIFE SKILL: #4. LETTING GO

25. JUST YOU 'N' ME 107
26. I TRUST ME 111
27. SUPERHERO 115
28. WONDER TWINS 119
29. A MOOSE ON THE DUNES 123
30. THE RUNAWAY GUITAR 127
31. ONCE SEVENTEEN 131
32. PINK PAUSES 135

LIFE SKILL: #5. BEING LOVING & RESPECTFUL

33. TOADS AND DIAMONDS 141
34. CARROTS DON'T HOP 143
35. A MOST GRACIOUS GUEST 147
36. THE MIDNIGHT MESSAGE 151
37. MAGIC HUGS 155
38. OH, IT WAS NOTHING 159
39. TUCKED INTO YOUR POCKET 163
40. JUST IN CASE YOU'RE STARVING 165

LIFE SKILL: #6. LOOKING FOR THE BIG PICTURE

41. LIKE THE BIG DIPPER 171
42. BROCCOLI FOR BREAKFAST 175
43. I'D RATHER VACUUM THAN FLOSS 179
44. SLOUCHING 183
45. DON'T START 185
46. THOUGHTS ON FIRE 187
47. CRUNCHY AIR 193
48. CHOCOLATE MELTS 197

LIFE SKILL: #7. WATCHING WHICH WAY WE'RE GOING

49. BEING WITH 205
50. NOT WITHOUT THAT CHICKEN 209
51. WHO'S WEARING MY RAINCOAT? 213
52. WHO HAD TOAST? 217
53. BUTTER ON YOUR ELBOW 221
54. THINKING DRINKING 223
55. MAIL PLANE 227
56. WHERE'S THE MOOSE? 231

LIFE SKILL: #8. LISTENING WITHIN

57. CUCUMBERS IN HER PURSE 235
58. UNA SIESTA 239
59. AH-CHOO! 243
60. BLACK ICE 247
61. SO NOT OK 251
62. THE BEST IN ME 255
63. OL' COOT 257
64. ALL DRESSED UP AND NOWHERE TO SNEEZE 261

LIFE SKILL: #9. TAKING ONE STEP AT A TIME

65. A REMOTE FOR KIDS 269
66. PICKED BY ME 273
67. WHAT'S IN A NAME? 277
68. CHANGING A TIRE WITHOUT SUPERMAN 281
69. WHAT'S BEHIND DOOR #3? 285
70. DO I REALLY NEED IT? 289
71. A BANANA PEEL 293
72. OVER THE EDGE 297

LIFE SKILL: #10. BEING POSITIVE

73. A HAPPY BED 303
74. THE MOTORCYCLE AND THE WIND 305
75. BATMAN'S BIRTHDAY 307
76. LOOKS LIKE CHICKEN GREASE 309
77. MAGIC HANDS 313
78. PARTY FOR ONE 315
79. MOM AT THE MET 319
80. A MAGIC CARPET RIDE 323
81. A BLUE EGG 327

IN AN EGGSHELL 331

A Very Short Intro

LIFE, I BELIEVE, IS MADE UP OF LITTLE MOMENTS.

Some we remember with big smiles.

Others we'd rather skip over.

Some we treasure, hoping never to forget.

Others we strive never to repeat.

Yet all moments become brighter when we recognize their wisdom within.

It only takes being conscious.

The idea for this book came to me as teenage mothers and high school students who I'd worked with during my master's in psychological counseling in New York City, were hugging me goodbye. The kids asked me to *leave* them with something. Would I please write down the stories I'd shared growing up as an only girl with four brothers in the rural Midwest in the sixties and seventies? They wanted something to refer back to concerning the life skills we'd practiced together like holding the peace, looking for the big picture, and letting go.

Growing up in a bustling, loving, close-knit family of seven, each of us with distinct and vibrant personalities, life wasn't always idyllic. Yet looking back, amid the organized chaos, I realized that I have very specific memories that illuminate the most poignant and harmonious moments of significance and brightness in my life that shaped my upbringing and transition into adulthood. They are moments that contributed the most positively to my physical, emotional, and inner well-being.

Dad was a painter and university professor turned multimedia producer. Mom was a writer and editor. We five kids spent as much time growing up in the studio at home amid mountains of photographic equipment and projectors as outside weeding in the vegetable garden or playing down in the woods.

While my stories are deeply personal, the life lessons strive to transcend my individual experiences, as emotions of uncertainty, anticipation, loss, and joy are universally relatable and shared by everyone.

Still, I'm glad that I've never had a crystal ball.

Because if I had *known* how long and winding the road would be from the idea…to *this* moment writing down its last words… well, I might have taken a different path.

But then you'd have nothing to have and hold.

(Or listen to.)

And refer back to.

Or share by reading aloud.

And I'm so happy you're here.

You and me and these stories.

I offer them with my whole heart's love.

I hope they bring you gifts of insight.

And little moments of joy.

—WENDY CLAIRE MANGEANT

(MARCH 5, 2024, MINNESOTA, USA)

LIFE SKILL

#1. Holding the Peace

Builds Calm

1.

Hold the Peace

AMAZINGLY, THERE WAS HARDLY ANY BLOOD.

I was dragging a big plastic garbage bag across the driveway when suddenly, I felt something squishy in my left tennis shoe. I pulled up my jeans and thought, *Wow, that's the inside of my leg.* I had unknowingly sliced it open on a broken piece of glass in the trash. I was fourteen.

The next moment, my brain came to a fork in the road. There were two ways in which I could go: I could panic or hold the peace.

I sat down on the driveway and called for Mom. She dashed out of the house and when she saw the gash in my leg, she froze, but only for an instant.

"Well, sweetie," Mom said, quietly exhaling her involuntary gasp. "I see you're already holding the peace, so I don't have to

remind you." She patted me on the shoulder and I managed a faint smile.

We kids had been taught by Mom and Dad, that in any kind of a crisis—a shock, bad news, an accident—to stop ourselves midaction, midemotion, midthought. Before anything else, we learned to pause in an upsetting situation, by mindfully taking several slow, deep breaths. To be in control of our emotions. If we were panicking, we couldn't think straight. If we were hysterical, those around us would have to calm us down before they could take care of the real problem.

Later that day, after our trip home from the hospital where I got fourteen stitches in my leg, Mom admitted that although she'd appeared calm on the outside when she first saw me, her brain had been processing a mile a minute. She said she'd been assessing if the wound would start gushing at any moment. But seeing I was in control of my feelings, she felt she could leave me to call for help.

We talked a little about the pattern of pausing to be peaceful, and she told me a story of being a brand-new mom and crossing the room to pick up her crying baby. My godmother had seen she was hurrying with worry, instead of picking up the baby peacefully.

It was then that twenty-four-year-old Mom began to learn that emotions emit actual vibrations and why being calm was so important. That no matter how loudly a baby is crying, eventually, they'll pick up on peaceful vibrations, too, and feeling safe, quiet down.

Fast forward to the five of us kids. Learning to hold the peace didn't mean we never got upset when we got hurt. Iain broke his nose. I ripped open my hand climbing a fence. Bruce got appendicitis. Douglas slipped on a frozen pond and split open his tiny chin. Christopher was stung stepping on an entire nest of yellow jackets and almost stopped breathing. But what mattered most when we got hurt, although we may have cried, is that we didn't go crazy. We'd been taught to stay calm in a crisis, so we could think straight.

There was the time Iain spilled a pot of boiling water from the stove on top of himself, and I remember Dad sprinting down the hallway with Iain in his arms, leaping into the shower, and spraying cold water on him still dressed. Thus, I learned that pausing didn't mean standing still and not reacting. I'd never seen Dad move so fast, and thinking straight, what he needed to do was move at the speed of light.

Driving back to college my sophomore year, the hood of my car suddenly unhinged and flew up, covering my windshield and completely obstructing my view. I don't remember thinking. I only remember braking evenly and pulling over to the side of the freeway which thankfully, was clear. My friend in the passenger seat asked in disbelief, "How did you do that?" I shook my head, not knowing, and burst into tears. Looking down in the rearview mirror that had landed in my lap, I thanked Life for keeping me safe, and Mom and Dad for helping me build the pattern of holding the peace that had worked automatically in a crisis.

But one of the times when staying calm mattered the most was when Mom and I were staying at my grandfather's old, weathered cottage on a tiny island in Canada. I was in a room that had been recently painted, and soon began to have trouble breathing. Minutes later, I was wheezing so badly, I was hardly able to inhale and found myself gasping for breath.

And I began to panic.

Panicking, I felt a shock wave of adrenaline explode through my body which terrified me. Then I remembered what I'd been taught. "Hold the peace, hold the peace," I repeated.

Suddenly, I got a clear inner message: *stand up*.

I struggled to my feet and the moment I did, something released in my chest, and I could inhale in slow motion.

Mom, down the hall on the phone with the paramedics, who were now instructing the ferry to turn around and head back to the island for me, instructed me to go into the bathroom, run hot water in the sink, and put my head over it covered with a towel to breathe in the steam.

By the time the ambulance arrived, I didn't need the oxygen tanks, but I put the mask on anyway because it seemed to help Mom breathe better. Later, the medic told me that staying upright was the best position for troubled breathing.

Interesting. Life had known. Not me.

Who knows? Perhaps the next time there's a crisis, I may be needed to sprint somewhere. If I am, I hope I can do it mindfully, reinforcing the message to my muscles to stay calm, so I can think straight.

To hold the peace instead of panic.

So I can listen. On the inside.

Stay calm in a crisis to think clearly.

2.

Pat-Pat

PAT-PAT, PAT-PAT.

What fun, I thought, holding the warm bundle in my arms and patting the back of my three-month-old godson. His mother had just nursed him, I had burped him, and now I was swaying from side to side to help him fall asleep. The problem was, he was as lively as a blue jay, eyes wide open, taking in everything as we did laps between the window and his crib. Meanwhile, his mother slipped farther down into the bean bag chair on the floor.

Softly I began to sing, but a few minutes later, it was only his mom's breathing that had changed. Pretty good for a little guy who'd taken a cable car to a nearby mountain top for a picnic that day, the exact reason why his mom and I were exhausted.

I tried again to lay him down in the crib, but the moment he was off my warm chest, he began to cry. No doubt his mom would have let him fuss knowing that finally, babies have to soothe themselves to sleep. But since I didn't get to see him very much, she let me spoil him a bit. So once again, I began pat-patting his little back.

Standing in the fading light, I began remembering the gentle pats that Mom and Dad had given to comfort me when I was sad or upset or had hurt myself. Offering me pats let me know I wasn't alone…they were there…it'll be OK…pat-pat.

As I felt my godson's head grow heavy in my arms, I stopped patting and instantly, he woke back up. Patting again, his eyes began to close.

Hmm.

After several failures to get him into the crib without crying—but waking up his mom—giddy from exhaustion, I limboed down to the floor with him on my chest. Then lying on my back, I started pushing with my feet and sliding along the floor toward the crib, so he got used to being quiet in a horizontal position. Then I slithered upright and deftly rolled him off my chest and into the crib. Of course, as soon as he touched the cold mattress, he woke back up and started crying again.

But I was already in position.

"There, there, you're fine," I cooed softly, gently patting him on the back again, and a few minutes later, he was sound asleep.

Lingering a moment longer, watching the blanket rise and fall with his every breath, I thought about what a little thing a pat is…how silently, yet sincerely it can offer comfort in all sorts of situations with family, friends, and colleagues…even with strangers. Offered respectfully when appropriate, a pat might be a little thing, but what a big message it can send: You're not alone. It's OK. I'm here. Be at peace.

Pat-pat.

Offer pats for comfort.

3.

All Tucked In

"YOU'RE A PRUNE," I SAID, LOOKING AT DOUGLAS'S wrinkled hands. It was the third time I'd returned to remind him it was time to get out of the bathtub. But he was decked out in a face mask and flippers and seemed happy, though the water had long ago gone cold. I pulled my ace: "Make it snappy and I'll read you and Moosie a bedtime story." He gurgled through his snorkel, and I knew we had a deal. Having been tucked into bed when I was small, continuing the tradition felt natural to me.

I remember Mom reading me stories at the end of the day in a white wooden rocking chair, and then sitting quietly on the bed and giving my tiny back a tiny massage to help me be relaxed before falling asleep. Then she'd pull up the covers, tuck the sheets under my chin, and kiss me goodnight. Dad gave goodnight hugs, too, but mostly my memories of being tucked in are of Mom.

Being six and eight years older than my little brothers, I often felt like I had live dolls to play with. On my own, I happily volunteered to run their baths with bubbles, shampoo their hair, zip them into Cookie Monster jammies with feet, carry them on my back to say goodnight to Mom and Dad, and read them bedtime stories to help quiet them down before bedtime. Then, I'd give each one a little back massage and kiss them goodnight.

When we kids were older, of course, we put ourselves to bed, and by high school, our homework lasted way past Mom and Dad's bedtime. In fact, I remember times when Dad would peek into my room having seen my light on in the middle of the night, checking to see if I was OK, reminding me that there was no point in taking an exam I couldn't wake up for.

Living on my own now, I see that a little routine has come into being as to how I quiet down my thoughts from a busy day. I usually light a candle, make herbal tea, maybe nibble on a cookie or a piece of toast, write in my journal, and do a tiny day review. Then one evening it occurred to me that this was me tucking myself in for bedtime.

Still, it made me smile the last time I was home visiting and found Mom sitting on the bed, waiting for me after my shower.

"I don't know if you're too old to be tucked in," she began.

"Never," I interrupted, slipping under the covers.

"Good," she continued, "because I wanted to offer you a little massage. It's hard to reach your back when it's in Spain."

Have a peaceful bedtime routine.

4.

Where Would I Be If I Were a Passport?

"GOT YOUR PASSPORT?" IAIN ASKED, ZOOMING UP TO the curb at JFK, popping on the hazard lights, and leaping from the car.

I froze.

"My passport," I repeated numbly. "Iain, I have absolutely no idea where my passport is. I didn't think about it once while packing."

I had just graduated from graduate school, was leaving for Spain that night, and the thought of not boarding the plane made me sweat. "I don't even know where to begin looking," I choked, knowing I was already late.

"OK," Iain said, taking a deep breath for me. "We're going to hold the peace while you try to picture the last time you had it. Where were you traveling to or from?" But feeling emotionally overwhelmed, I couldn't think straight. In fact, in that particular moment, I couldn't think at all. Iain put his hand on my shoulder, reminding me that he was there.

"All right," I said, trying not gulp air. "New Year's. No, wait, a few months ago when I traveled on a mail plane."

"Good," Iain said. "Go back to that trip."

I sat down on the curb, consciously slowing my breath to calm down, all the while knowing that an airport clock was ticking somewhere and the space between now and my boarding time was shrinking. I closed my eyes, trying to "see" my passport. Nothing. My mind was a blank.

Suddenly, I heard myself say, "Where would I be, if I were a passport?" and the next thing I knew, my hand pointed, Ouija-style, to a cardboard box Iain had taped shut sitting next to my two suitcases. It held my computer in a soft case wrapped in a down comforter for the journey home.

Iain took out the small knife he always carried—just like Dad—and sliced the box open. My hand, seemingly with a mind of its own, unzipped the outer pocket of the computer case, and pulled out my passport.

"Ta da!" Iain said, beaming.

"I don't believe it," I said in astonishment. "I had no idea where it was." Then Iain whipped out a roll of tape from his backpack and began securing the box again. "How'd you know we'd need that?" I asked, eyeing him suspiciously.

"It's weird, but this roll of tape *told* me to bring it along," he said, shrugging his shoulders. "Funny how that works sometimes." But in that moment, it didn't seem funny at all. "Thank you—thank you," I said, hugging my big brother goodbye. "For everything. But mostly for helping me hold the peace. I wouldn't be going home tonight if it weren't for you."

"Oh, that's OK," Iain said, heaving my things onto a nearby cart. "I'm coming with you. One of these suitcases has my things in it," he joked.

Watching the tiny lights below disappear as the plane rose

into the sky, I went back to the moment of finding my passport. I couldn't help thinking that Life had known where it was all along, and by being calm, I had had a better chance of being led in the right direction.

It gave me something to think about for a long time: the idea that on some cosmic level, from Life's point of view anyway, nothing is ever really...lost.

I must have found the idea quite comforting because I fell sound asleep rising up over Long Island and woke up in Spain.

Know where important documents are.

5.

The Flaming Sword

IT WAS A MOMENT I'LL NEVER FORGET.

Dad was in his studio squeezing twelve new tubes of paint into a palette he took traveling that looked like half a plastic egg carton. When it was full, he handed me the case and asked me to carry it to the other side of the room to lay on a table. And because it had cute little handles, I folded the case closed, snapping the handles together, and carried it like the tiny suitcase it looked like.

"Just leave it open in the sunshine so the colors can dry," Dad added without looking up, "otherwise they'll run."

And my heart skipped a beat.

With trembling hands, I unsnapped the handles, opened the case, and saw a very colorful collage.

What had my eleven-year-old brain been thinking?

I wanted to disappear. Right where I stood.

Just go *poof*.

Dad was going to be so mad.

I took a deep breath, remembering to tell the truth and hope for the best.

"Daddy," I said, clearing my throat.

"Hmm," he hummed, beginning to fill the second case.

"I'm so sorry," I said, meaning it sincerely, "but I've ruined your new paints. Please forgive me." And I showed him the paints still slowly running together.

And I'll never forget what he did.

Absolutely nothing.

He just looked at the colorful mess and sighed.

But not even an upset sigh.

And the fact that Dad didn't get upset turned that moment into a *teaching* moment for me.

I'm serious.

If an angel with a flaming sword had appeared out of the blue, I couldn't have been more astonished than I was by Dad's grace.

"I forgive you, sweetheart," he said simply. "After all, you didn't do it on purpose."

And that was that.

Then he handed me the second travel case with its twelve newly poured colors to lay in the sunshine to dry. Tiptoeing across the room with it, I could hardly believe my luck. Looking back at Dad scraping the brand-new colors I'd ruined into the trash, I thought my heart would burst with gratitude.

At the fork in the road—the one that I like to imagine appears when things don't go as we plan or hope—Dad chose the high road.

He held the peace.

That moment teaches me *still*.

Forgive with grace.

6.

Squish, Squish

SQUISH, SQUISH, SQUISH.

"Slow down or you're gonna regret it," I said severely to myself in the bathroom mirror. "Do it with grace or not at all." I squished back to the bedroom, having stepped on the wet bathroom mat wearing only one tennis shoe, not having found its mate yet. Racing around the house was so unfair to Frédéric and Mom and Dad, because seeing someone rushing can be very anxiety-producing. Even I didn't want to be around me.

But there I was, whirling wildly around like the Tasmanian She Devil—minus the red lipstick and heels—stuffing things last minute into my suitcase; banging my knee on the bed frame; catching my shirtsleeve on the door handle; and knocking over my tea, soaking the boarding passes.

Taking this as a sign, I sat down to pause.

Sitting still to re-center, I also hoped I'd get a leading as to where my missing tennis shoe was, praying it wasn't in the two-hundred-pound suitcase Frédéric had just wrestled upstairs and already put into the car.

As I sat in neutral, it occurred to me that I'd obviously forgotten some things that I thought I'd already learned and did by default. One was packing the day before the last day of vacation. That way, the last day still feels like vacation, and you only have to tuck your jammies and toothbrush into the top of your suitcase, zip it closed, and waltz out the door. A second thing was getting a good night's sleep before traveling the next day. Having not done that and packing past midnight, so only sleeping four hours, I felt like I wanted to puke. Plus with less sleep, I knew my immune system would be weaker, making me more susceptible to the goobies carried by fellow travelers who'd also been up too late packing, so now I'd probably get sick.

A third thing I regretted was forgetting to do the most important things first on vacation. On day one, Mom had asked if we could go for a paddleboat ride. I said, "Sure, we have plenty of time." But then the days went by and before I knew it, it was the last morning of the last day and the normally clear blue Minnesota sky was...green. Then the wind began to howl, the waves put on little white caps, and there was no way Mom and I could go. We'd capsize. Thoroughly disappointed in myself, I hoped we'd get another chance the following summer, but my heart was heavy knowing that we never know the future.

Then I spied my other tennis shoe.

Hiding under Frédéric's side of the bed.

I'd have never seen it if I hadn't sat down to pause.

"Gracefully," I reminded myself aloud, exchanging my soggy sock for a dry one and slipping on my tennis shoe.

Gratefully, moving more peacefully, I was fully awake hugging and kissing Mom and Dad goodbye, whereas in the past, I had sometimes rushed through that, too, missing the entire moment.

Amazingly enough, the next summer, my first morning home in Minnesota, the lake's surface was without a ripple. I tiptoed into the kitchen to make a surprise picnic breakfast. Then I invited Mom to come down to the lake under the pretense of watching the sunrise together from the shore. Standing on the dock, I told her, in fact, we were going for a paddleboat ride, only uncovering the breakfast basket when we were floating in the middle of the lake.

I'd made a little fruit salad of strawberries, watermelon, peaches, and blueberries; toasted English muffins, cold but still crunchy; brought butter and jam; and filled my water bottle with orange juice.

As the first rays of the sun appeared through the trees, the shore behind us turned deep gold. A fish jumped and a loon started calling, and I started pretending that I was conducting Mother Nature's symphony, bringing in each new sound. Then silence descended once again, and as Mom and I floated in the middle of the lake making a memory together, well, it felt a lot like grace.

Arrive and depart with grace.

7.

Whoosh!

"HI, YOU HOME?" FRÉDÉRIC ASKED, BREATHLESS OVER the phone.

"I'm here," I said calmly.

"I forgot the keys to a building I'm showing to an important client this morning on my desk. Can you bring them to me?" He was near the Prado Museum in the center of Madrid.

I looked at myself in the bathroom mirror, still in my pajamas, having sat down for a moment to read over a story—and two hours later, I was still editing.

"I'll leave in the next sixty seconds," I said, my heart already speeding up.

"OK, but be safe," he said.

"Of course," I said, automatically.

But I wasn't really listening.

I was already in a hurry.

I pulled on leggings and a sweatshirt, skipped the bra, jammed my feet into still-tied tennis shoes, then nearly broke my neck as I hopped on one foot down the stairs trying to unlace them so I could drive the car, grabbing the handrail to break my fall.

I raced out the door, screeched out of the driveway, then nearly clipped a tree going around a corner, looking down for a split second for the mints in the glove compartment since I hadn't brushed my teeth. I planned on brushing my hair at the first red light, and maybe even surreptitiously slipping on my bra that I'd stuffed in my purse.

I went slowly enough through the neighborhood to became only slightly airborne over the speed bumps and careened onto the freeway.

Suddenly, I heard Mom's voice say, "Careful rushing, babe," as clearly as if she'd been in the backseat instead of Minneapolis. I glanced into the rearview mirror anyway.

One whoosh and you could be gone.

Especially in a car.

Accidents weren't planned.

I consciously slowed down.

As luck would have it, rush hour was over and I sailed into the city and pulled neatly up to Frédéric waving gratefully from the sidewalk, rolled down my window, and reached to hand him the—OMG.

"I…I…," I stuttered.

"Forgot the keys," he said, shaking his head and looking up to the heavens. He sighed, pulling out his phone to call the client, and I sat there dumbfounded at my utter idiocy. For all my mindfulness training, I hadn't taken one moment to pause, to center myself, before moving into action.

Once, I rushed out the door late for the airport, only to leave my passport back at Mom and Dad's on the breakfast table, and going back for it, missed my plane.

Another time, I raced up the stairs so I wouldn't be late for class, spilling hot chocolate down my front, so I had to change, missing more of my lecture.

Still another time, being late for a dinner party, I was putting on mascara while walking, and I walked directly into a glass door that was normally open in the hallway. Needless to say, I didn't need any eye shadow that night, as my left eyelid slowly turned dark blue throughout the evening. I'm only lucky I didn't need stitches.

See a pattern here?

Rushing didn't save me any time at all; in fact, moving without calm usually made me later. Funny how Life has a way of giving us the same lesson repeatedly in different scenarios, I suppose hoping we learn it.

Gratefully, Frédéric changed his appointment for later that day and I drove humbly home, retrieved the keys, and drove back to him almost in slow motion.

Once back home a second time, I turned off the car engine and just sat there in the car thinking about the consequences of my mindless actions. Acknowledging my tendency to rush, I realized that only by letting go of my belief that doing things faster felt more productive, would I be free to move with a new kind of mindfulness.

Whooshing, I could never be calm.

Not being calm, I was bound to miss things.

Rushing in the wrong direction, I could potentially become something others would miss.

A very sobering thought.

Then my cell phone rang.

"Hi, you home?" Frédéric asked.

"I'm here," I replied, newly grounded.

"Good," he said. "That's all that matters."

Because accidents aren't planned.

One whoosh and you could be gone.

Beware of rushing.

8.

Always the Sky

I REMEMBER A MOMENT WHEN I WAS REALLY NOT OK.
And I felt like doing something.
Slightly drastic.
Like screaming.
But then I remembered that screaming should really be saved for an emergency. Like a fire. Or being in an accident. Or mortal danger.
Which I wasn't.
I thought about breaking something.
Like dishes.
But then they'd be broken.
I thought about yelling.
But I always regretted raising my voice at someone. And I know how I feel when someone yells at me.
I could talk to someone. Someone who cared.
That usually helped.
But I was alone and didn't feel like talking to anyone.
Not yet.
Then I thought, *Well, I could breathe.*

Not normal breath breathing, but mindful breathing. Something to help me through this not OK moment.

And then the sky called me...

So I snuck outside.

And looking up into it, I began slowly inhaling while counting to five...then held my breath for five...and slowly exhaled for five.

Huh.

Then I put my palms together in front of my heart and slowly breathed a full breath again.

And I feel a tiny bit better.

I do.

And now taking a few more breaths, I'm remembering how blessed conscious breathing is.

Like a bridge over an upset moment.

And now here I am on the other side.

A little more peaceful. A little more OK.

Thank heavens, there's always the sky.

Hmm.

Being under the open sky can calm.

LIFE SKILL

#2. Believing in the Process

Builds Patience

9.

Thump-Thump

A LONE STAR APPEARED IN THE SUNSETTING SKY, BUT it was too late to wish upon it. I was already holding the envelope that would tell me if I'd been accepted to graduate school or not. It felt kinda thin.

I opened the envelope.

I wasn't accepted.

I stood blankly at a fork in the road that appeared in my mind. I imagined a signpost with different pairs of words pointing in opposite directions. PANIC–PEACEFUL. FREAK OUT–YOU'RE FINE. DESPAIR–WHAT IF?

I inhaled and exhaled for a few deep breaths, letting the news of my present moment sink in. *Well, now you have no flipping idea what you'll be doing for the next two years*, a thought zipped by. *Probably should've applied to more than one school*, came another. *What...the...heck?* unfolded a third. *Now what?*

Then my eyes refocused on the sky turning to dusk, and seeing the tiny light of a single star, I surprised the me that is behind my eyes and sighed with a small sigh. I reminded myself that I believe in Life's process swirling and whirling to sustain and maintain the balance of all things.

I didn't have to remind it to use the oxygen I'd just inhaled. I had faith in the processes already worked out to do those things. Busy making new galaxies on the other side of the Universe, Life hadn't forgotten about tiny me. I placed my hand over my heart for reassurance...*thump-thump, thump-thump*...yep, still beating.

OK...well...what next? I wondered. *Should I call Mom and Dad?*

No, was the feeling I got. *Wait a while. They may ask questions you're not ready to answer yet. Sit with the news by yourself a bit. Life is always a few steps ahead. Eventually, you'll see which way to move.*

I knew it was rarely a clear understanding of what to do next, but more a feeling that this way was better to go than that way.

This step better than that step.

Tip tip toe.

A harvest moon began to rise and I thought about how each moment unfolds from the wholeness of the moment before.

Of course, a next step would unfold itself.

Just like flowers do.

Wouldn't I have smiled if I'd known that by not getting into the University of Minnesota that fall, I'd move back home for a full year to work in Mom and Dad's media business, and earn and save enough money to go backpacking with a friend through Europe the following spring. A few days into our trip where we planned to travel through sixteen countries, I met my soulmate crossing the street in our first town in Spain.

And I'm still here.

(But that's another story.)

Still, whenever I'm feeling discouraged not knowing which way to turn, I try to remember to put my hand over my heart to feel its faithful rhythm...*thump-thump...thump-thump...* reminding me of Life's taking-care process and that I've not been forgotten. Of course, a next step will appear, just as the word "evolution" is derived from the Latin meaning *unrolling*.

There's always a further way to go...

I just need to be patient.

Remember that Life is a process.

10.

Potatoes with Pa

THE SUMMER I TURNED EIGHT, OUR FAMILY PLANTED a giant vegetable garden. Working those long, muggy days hoeing, seeding, watering, and weeding, I thought it covered maybe half of Ohio. Dad began by churning the earth with the gasoline-powered red cultivator, while we kids worked up ahead at a safe distance, searching for and throwing any big stones we found to the side, wincing at the sound the rotating blades made when we missed one.

We planted row after row of different vegetables, lining one side of the garden with raspberries and another side with zinnia flowers. We had a small strawberry patch, planted corn in one corner and asparagus in another, and had one lone blueberry bush the blackbirds thought was just for them.

Bright green heads of lettuce were the first thing to magically appear, and I remember the fun of Dad asking me to run outside to carefully tear off seven leaves for seven BLTs that he was making for lunch. But as the warm weeks went by, coming back with my empty basket because no strawberries were ripe—so no shortcake for dessert—I began to be a little impatient.

"Well, it takes time for things to grow," Dad said, going back out to the patch with me one evening. "Think of what it takes for a little white flower to turn into a strawberry. We wouldn't want to rush the strawberries growing, just as we wouldn't rush you growing up," which, said like that, made sense to small me.

So, we learned to be patient as things grew, and grew, and GREW.

By midsummer, we had edible rainbows of green beans and asparagus, yellow squash and corn, orange zucchini blossoms and bell peppers, red tomatoes, pink watermelons, blueberries, and purple onions.

But as yummy as the garden was, it wasn't always fun to have one. In fact, most of the time after weeding the raspberries, tying up the tomatoes, and carrying heavy buckets of water to parts of the garden where the hose didn't reach, after an hour or so, I was ready to call it a day.

Once, Mom asked me to pick the green beans, so I did. A whole mixing bowl full. But thinking I was back inside the house too soon, she went out and spot-checked a row. Needless to say, I was sentenced back to the beginning of the first row to pick all the beans ready that day. By the time I was done, I could've sworn I'd been out there for a...month.

Another time, Mom and I were picking beans together, and since we were chatting, I hardly noticed what my hands were doing. But then she said, "OK, sweetie, I'm going inside to start dinner now. You can finish up, can't you?" and my heart sank as I watched her walk away. If I'd known she was going to leave me, I'd have worked faster with her company.

As each summer rolled around, it became a tradition that we'd all start working right after breakfast before things got really hot and muggy. But as long and sweaty and bug-slapping as those days were, they're also some of my happiest childhood memories.

I remember racing with Iain as we picked the raspberries...guessing with Bruce and Douglas how long a carrot would be before pulling it up...surprising Dad with blueberries the blackbirds hadn't gotten through the new net...cutting asparagus with Mom when it was as tall as a pencil...picking cucumbers with Christopher through my T-shirt to avoid the prickles I never knew they had until I grabbed one bare-handed...realizing that pickles were *baby* cucumbers...harvesting the acorn squash I didn't have to eat because Mom didn't like it either...and picking the broccoli I loved, but inspected from every angle before a bite, after Iain found a tiny green worm waving to him from his dinner fork, perfectly camouflaged on a floret.

But working day after day in the garden reminded us kids of where food really comes from, and instilled in me a great respect for nature—and a reverence for how it nurtured me.

But the best moments of all were finding potatoes with Pa.

One afternoon, Dad and I ran out to the garden as the sky was darkening, grinning like idiots because we both loved storms. Dad, with his trusty shovel, began lifting up clods of earth while I sifted through the soil with my hands, excitedly holding up every potato I found. We marveled at the big ones, laughed at the funny-shaped ones, and tucked the tiny ones back into the ground for more growing. Watching us from afar, you'd have thought we were digging up treasure.

Only now do I realize we were.

Our garden let us witness the wonder of Life's creative process up close. It was a process that unfolded so slowly, you could never see the exact moment when a blossom opened or a berry became ripe, yet that which wasn't ready at the end of the day, the next morning was.

Although, perhaps what grew up most in that garden…was us.

Grow a garden.

11.

F-r-e-d

IT WAS A PERFECT SUMMER DAY FOR PLAYING OUTSIDE, but Mom didn't care. Today, thirteen-year-old me was going to begin learning how to type properly, which meant not looking down at my fingers to find each letter on the keyboard. I rolled a fresh piece of paper into Mom's electric typewriter with a sigh. I thought of how Mom typed. She was so fast, her fingers were a blur.

"I'll never be able to do that," I told her, watching in amazement. "How do your fingers know where to go on their own?"

"With patience, they learn," Mom said, handing me the typing book. I wasn't sure, but I wasn't allowed to play outside until I'd done the first lesson. I flipped open the book, which stood up like a little A-frame house, and positioned it on my left.

"Hey, Mom," I called, "there's a picture of the keyboard on the first page. Can I look at that?"

"Of course, you can, Silly," she called back. "You have to learn where the letters are first."

Oh, this isn't going to be so bad, I thought, placing my left fingers on the home keys of *A, S, D,* and *F*, my right fingers on *J, K, L,* and the semicolon, and resting my thumbs on the space bar.

Then I copied *fgjh fgjh fgjh fgjh* using only my index fingers, making the spaces in between using my thumbs.

Then I typed three lines of *frf*, *juj*, *ded*, *kik*, and *sws*.

"Hey, Mom," I called about ten minutes later, "I just typed my first word! And I did it without looking at my fingers!" Mom came out of the kitchen to watch. "Look," I said, pressing down the letter *r* with my left index finger, then the *e* with my left middle finger, and the *d* below the *e*.

"R-e-d," I spelled out. "Red. Oh, and watch this, f-r-e-d. Fred." Mom grinned. I would have, too, if I'd known that I had just typed my husband-to-be's name sixteen years into the future, although his would have French accent marks over the *e*.

"Keep going," she said, returning to the kitchen. "Pretty soon you'll be as fast as I am." I doubted it, but I was going to try.

With every passing day, my fingers learned the locations of new letters. With each new letter, I made new words, and near the end of the summer, it happened. I was slowly typing the lesson from the book on my left when I realized that without looking, my fingers knew where to go on their own.

I was thrilled. I was also hooked.

It's hard to believe now that I learned to type on a typewriter without a delete key or automatic spellchecker. I even see a lot of people typing madly away on their computer keyboards, thinking they know how to type. But they're not typing sixty words a minute as breezily as I am, having to keep sneaking a peek at their fingers, even if they think they're not.

Apparently, their moms didn't have them stay inside for part of a summer learning how to type properly. How I wish I could lend them my typing book that still stands up like a little A-frame, then they'd know the freedom that comes with flying across the keyboard with fingers that know where to go on their own.

Learn to type without looking at your fingers.

12.

Not Ready Yet

ONE DAY WHEN I WAS AROUND FOURTEEN, THERE WAS an afternoon when I was in my bedroom feeling particularly fragile, and there was only one thing I wanted to do. Go find Mom. Like a heat-seeking missile, I went straight to where I knew she would be and knocked on her office door.

"Come in," said Mom.

"Is the doctor in?" I asked, making a mopey face.

"She certainly is," she said, looking up from her blue typewriter, her face lighting up at my question. "And there's nothing more she'd rather do than talk with you." Then she pulled up a second chair, and I started sharing the goings-on in my teenage head about how big the world looked outside my window, and how scary it was knowing I'd be going out into it one day.

"So, I've decided that I'm never leaving home, ever," I said, crawling uninvited onto her lap, my adolescent legs overflowing to the floor. "I'm going to stay here with you and Dad. I like it here." Mom started laughing but put her arms around me anyway.

"Sweetheart," she said, "there's a moment for everything. Now is the time to be home, but getting you ready to leave the nest may be the most important part of parenting, and one day, I promise, you'll be happy to leave, because you'll be ready. You're just not ready *yet*." And we talked about being patient with the process, and how things unfold in their own time.

Walking back to my bedroom after our talk, it was strange to realize that nothing had changed out in the world, but things had changed in my head, which made all the difference.

Once again, lying on my bed and looking out my window at the apple tree beyond, I remembered that not long ago, it had been covered in pink blossoms. Now the blossoms had given way to tiny apples, the size and color of green peas. In the fall, the apples would be red and ripe.

But they weren't ready yet.

Neither was I.

Four years later, just as Mom predicted, I was ready and excited to leave home for college. Four years after that, I was ready to leave the States to explore Europe. Four years after that, I was ready to move to Spain and begin a new chapter in my life in a new culture and language.

I was twenty-six.

I hadn't been ready a moment before, but I was ready now, grateful there's a moment for everything.

There's a moment for everything.

13.

Par Lay Voo Fran Say?

"FRAISE," SAID MOM, HELPING ME STUDY FOR MY sixth-grade French quiz.

"Strawberry," I said.

"Good. And how do you spell it?" she asked. I looked at her blankly.

"Oh, we don't have to know how to spell the words, only what they mean," I replied.

"What do you mean, you don't have to know how to spell the words?" she asked.

"Our teacher just puts all the French words on one side of the page, the English ones on the other side, mixed up, and you match them," I said simply.

"But what if you want to write the word one day?" Mom asked.

I shrugged my shoulders. "She said to study the vocabulary at the end of the chapter. I've studied it. That makes me done." Mom raised an eyebrow.

"Try," she suggested.

"Fine," I said. "F-r-a-i-s-e."

"Parfait," said Mom with a French accent I didn't know she could do. "Apple."

"Huh?" I said.

"Apple," she repeated.

"Oh, we don't have to know them that way," I said. "I only studied them from French to English." Mom put the book down and looked at me thoughtfully.

"Honey," she began, "I know learning French isn't that much fun, but one day, you'll want to visit France, right?"

"I suppose so," I said, having never thought about it before.

"Of course you will," she said brightly. "You'll want to see Paris, look out from the top of the Eiffel Tower, and see Monet's lilies up close with your own eyes." I knew this was true, having seen them in Dad's art books. "Imagine one day, you can speak French and order food from a menu. Who knows? You might even make a new friend there. That's the fun of traveling."

"But learning vocabulary is so boring," I moaned.

"Well, then," said Mom patiently, "let's make it more fun by changing the context. Let's pretend you're at a local market buying an apple. You don't want to just point your finger. How would you say apple, see voo play?"

"Une pomme," I said. "P-o-m-m-e."

"Mais oui," said Mom. "And apple of the ground?"

"Pomme de terre," I answered easily, "potato." And on we went, imagining I was in France, which I had to admit, made it a bit more fun.

Well, lo and behold, the next day's quiz was fill-in-the-blank and as I wrote in the words that I had practiced spelling with Mom, I couldn't stop blessing her.

Little did I dream that crossing a street one day, near the border between France and Spain, I'd hear a beautiful foreign voice beside me speaking English, which caused me to turn my head. He was French, and I'm sure that I used up all the vocabulary I learned in school in the first twelve minutes of our conversation.

Thankfully, Frédéric had studied a lot harder than I had, and taken learning a foreign language more seriously, because afterward, we were able to have a real conversation in English. And one conversation led to another, and then another.

And four years later, we were married.
I think it was his accent.

Learn to speak a foreign language.

14.

My Happy List

ONE LATE MORNING, I FOUND MOM BACK IN BED FEELing out of sorts, so I gave her a hug and reminded her that she was my favorite mom in the whole world. She tried to smile, but I could tell she was only pretending.

"OK," I said, sitting down, seeing I needed to be the mom in that moment. "I'm going to remind you of something that you once shared with me. Ready? Here it is." I picked up her hand for effect. "Whatever you're feeling this moment, it's valid. It's simply how you're feeling. *But this, too, will pass.* I promise. You won't always feel this way. Life is change and then more change. And if you're willing to be a little bit patient, you'll find that with time, your feelings will have changed too. For the better," I added, and Mom squeezed my hand in acknowledgment.

"In the meantime," I continued, "tell me something that makes you happy. Something small. Something possible right now, and we'll take it from there."

She thought for a moment.

"Maybe a little shoulder massage," she said, and I picked up the phone and pretended to order one. After giving her a little massage, she seemed a bit less mopey.

"That'll be $12.40," I said. "Plus tax."

"I'll get my purse," she muffled into her pillow. Then I coaxed her off the bed, and we went into her home office to keep talking about how she was feeling. Then I had an idea. I told her that at college, I'd written something in my journal called My Happy List. It was a list of simple things that made me happy to help me through a fragile moment. Then I suggested that we each make a list, and mine went something like this:

MY HAPPY LIST:
- toast with butter
- going for a walk
- listening to the wind in the trees
- candlelight
- having a good talk
- journal writing
- thunderstorms
- reading a good book
- naps
- hot chocolate
- homemade cookies
- hugs
- cake
- birds singing

After we read our lists aloud, we went to have hot chocolate and go for a walk, two items we had in common.

Within five minutes of walking, Mom's mood began to change. Maybe it's about getting your bod up and out the door and some extra movement in your bloodstream that helps lumpy or bumpy feelings begin to change. But whatever it is, there seems to be something healing in the act of walking. Someone said once that if you have a problem, go for a walk. If you still have the problem at the end, go for another walk. I can't tell you how many times that's worked for me.

Mom and I talked the whole time during our walk, stopping only to listen to the wind and the birds in the trees. Together, under the open sky, Mom's vibration began to shift. Once back home, she thanked me with a hug, saying how different she felt and that she was ready to get back to her desk.

Our happy lists had worked.

About an hour later, I peeked into her office, and saw she was typing merrily away, so I didn't disturb her. But I did notice that her happy list was now tacked on her bulletin board above her desk. I smiled seeing it in plain view, knowing that now I could easily sneak a peek during a future fragile moment.

When a mom might need a little lift.

Up.

Remember simple things that make you happy.

15.

Brighter in the Morning

I NEVER KNEW CALCULATORS COULD BE SO SCARY.

It was Friday night, which usually felt like the friendliest part of the week, so I decided it was a good moment to be brave and began totaling up my student loans from college. Then I added on my present loan for graduate school. Then the interest I'd pay if I needed all the months, in all the years, in all three coupon books. Then I added that to my current monthly bills.

Then I started to have trouble breathing.

I needed Mom.

"Hello?" Mom said, sounding as if she were down the hall instead of halfway across the country.

"Mom?" I croaked but got no further. While I sniffed and snuffled telling her that I didn't see how I was going to make it financially, make it ever, she just listened, quietly saying, "There, there," and "It'll be all right," in all the right places until I was calm again.

It'd been worth calling just for that.

Then we talked about what I might need for short-term financial balance—maybe she needed to offer me a short-term loan—and we talked a bit more about the bigger picture, but honestly, I don't remember the details. I only remember her making room for my feelings—irrational or not—and reminding me of something I knew, but had temporarily forgotten.

"Sweetie," she said soothingly, "this is how you feel now, but it's been a long day and you're all out of energy. It's nighttime and it's dark outside your window, and perhaps that makes things seem scarier than they really are. But you don't have to decide anything tonight. Be patient. Just remember," she added, "things have a way of looking brighter in the morning. Just be good to yourself tonight."

"All right," I sniffed, feeling a smidgen better, if only because I'd been given permission to be good to myself tonight. "Thank you, Mom."

"Anytime," she said. "That's why I'm here. "

"Then can I also have a massage?" I asked, blowing my nose.

I was in New York.

Mom was in Minnesota.

"I'll be right over," she said.

The next morning, everything looked...different. *Brighter.*

My situation was the same, of course, but *I* was different.

Rested and refreshed, things looked newly possible, and I couldn't help acknowledging how hope seemed to arrive with the morning light.

I also remembered that Life unfolds one day at a time.

One moment at a time.

I could put my arms around that.

Because finally, no matter how dark or difficult a day feels, eventually it does come to an end. And with the sunrise, no matter the sky, things truly are brighter in the morning.

And morning always comes.

Things look brighter in the morning.

16.

Every Hundred Years

"I don't see your little Spanish village," she said, calling from Italy.

"OK," I said, cradling the phone between my shoulder and chin to better see my map of Europe. "It's right in the middle of the Pyrenees. On the south side. It's tiny."

"Oh, I found it," she said. "Tiny? It's a dot."

"You should talk," I laughed. "The only people who speak your town's dialect live in its valley. Are you sure you don't live in Brigadoon?"

"What's a Brigadoon?" she asked.

"Oh," I sighed dreamily, "it's a Hollywood musical where a little town called Brigadoon appears only once every hundred years. Gene Kelly falls in love with a girl from there and they dance on the hillside among the flowers. But then the town's about to disappear again for one hundred years, and you've got to see it. Your town looked like that the first time I saw it surrounded by the mountain mist. But back to us. Can you come?"

"I really want to," she said. "It's not enough to see you only once a year. I'll check plane fares on my end, you check there, and let's talk later this week." And we hung up, not wanting to spend our money talking long distance.

A few days later, I told her about a flight I'd found from Milan to Madrid with a stopover in Morocco. She told me about an overnight train from Bolzano to Barcelona.

I offered to parachute out of a small plane.

She offered to hire a hot air balloon.

I suggested she move to Spain.

She suggested we meet halfway in Paris.

I said, "Let's just go to Jamaica."

Then there was silence on the phone.

"It just doesn't seem to be a thing, does it?" I sighed.

"What do you mean?" she asked.

"It's a phrase my parents used when we kids wanted to do something. It helped us stay relaxed about things from the beginning and not get our hopes up too high. It means not forcing something to work out, just because you want it to, so things stay in balance."

"Hmm," she hummed, listening.

"Of course, we have to plan things," I continued. "It's just good to stay open and flexible, too, because sometimes Life shows you a different way to go than you originally thought."

"Oh, I know what you mean," she said. "Once I planned to go to a town an hour down the mountain pass, and suddenly, I got a feeling that I shouldn't go. It was so strange. I just sat there in the car all dressed up with this kind of warning. Finally, I turned the car around and stayed home. And guess what happened?"

"What?" I asked, curious.

"An ice storm came out of nowhere. No forecast or anything, and all the roads were closed. There were accidents everywhere. I'd have been stranded and unable to get back home if I'd gone."

"My friend and I used that phrase, 'if it's a thing,' almost daily, backpacking through Europe," I said. "Because sometimes things went along without a hitch, and other times, one thing after another went wrong. We'd miss the last train, the museum we'd traveled two days to see was closed, our hotel was full, and we'd have to just let everything go and come up with a new plan to go forward. So this feels like we're forcing it, doesn't it?"

"It does," she admitted. "And we both know there'll be a right time to see each other. We've found them in the past. Let's stay in touch and see what the future brings."

Sure enough, a few months later, she found a perfect flight she could afford without a parachute being a part of the price. But now a whole year has passed, and it's my turn to visit her. Now, she lives on the northern tip of Germany near an island called Hiddensee, which I can't even find on my map.

Oh, wait, here it is. It's a...dot.

Not going to be an easy trip from Madrid. Maybe I'll just have her press Start on her fax machine and I'll arrive that way.

But whatever it takes, I'll get there.

Even if the island appears only once every one hundred years, I'll get there.

When it's a thing.

Flowing works better than forcing.

LIFE SKILL

#3. Offering Feelings

Builds Balance

17.

Offering Feelings

When I was a little girl,
my godmother gave me a gift.
She taught me how to offer my feelings.
She helped me understand that whenever
I was feeling mad or sad or angry or frustrated,
those feelings had power in them,
which was a gift in Life's hands.
But held to myself, they could make me feel bad.
She said that feelings were signals,
and to acknowledge and explore them
to see what they were saying.
But once I had understood them,
to offer to let them go.
So when I was small, I practiced offering,
pretending I was a piece of Swiss cheese,
letting my upset feelings go right through the holes.
When I was a bit older,
I imagined placing my feelings into a picnic basket,
and leaving it on a hillside as a present.

When I went to college,
I began meditating and practiced mindful breathing.
I'd slowly re-center by inhaling,
letting go of my feelings while exhaling,
imagining them wafting away on the wind like dandelion seeds.
Because feelings once freed can transform
into positive energy with new purpose.
Perhaps to unfurl a leaf. Or ripen a peach.
But I'll leave the details in Life's hands.
I don't know why offering works,
I only know that it seems to.
And although I've never looked for a gift in return,
There often is one.
A little more peace.

Offering feelings builds balance.

18.

We Don't Bite

DOUGLAS, AGE TWO, WANTED THE DUMP TRUCK.

But Bruce, age four, was playing with it.

Douglas made a grab for it, tugged, but Bruce didn't let go.

Douglas swatted Bruce on his arm. *Fwap!*

Bruce still didn't let go.

So, Douglas leaned over and bit Bruce.

And Bruce let go.

I jumped off my swing midair, sailed to the ground, and headed for the sandbox.

"Douglas," I said, shaking my ten-year-old finger as I approached, "we don't hit, and we don't bite." Bruce, great tears welling up in his eyes, held up his forearm, showing me the teeth marks. I knelt down between them in the sand. This was a teaching moment. This is how they learned.

"Douglas," I repeated, looking directly at him, "we don't hit. Soft with our hands. Soft." And very gently, I picked up his hand and guided it to stroke my arm, reinforcing the principle that he was absolutely capable of understanding.

"And you know perfectly well that we don't bite. Ever," I

continued, in an unemotional but firm voice, conscious of how intelligent little kids really are. "You need to say you're sorry to Bruce." Douglas, a scowl on his face, looked from me to Bruce, who was still holding up his arm as if he'd been mortally wounded.

"Sorry," said Douglas, sulkily, not meaning it. I looked at him and raised my eyebrow, letting him know that he could do better, and that I wasn't going anywhere until he did. Douglas could already construct full sentences, and it was exactly moments like these where two-year-olds needed to be held accountable. No way were Mom and Dad raising wild kids. Romping around, fun-loving, spirited, lively kids, sure, but not wild. There were rules at home. Especially for moments like these.

"Sorry," Douglas repeated, maybe meaning it.

And Bruce...being Bruce...leaned over and kissed Douglas on the cheek.

This simple gesture utterly disarmed Douglas who, in response, hugged Bruce's head with his sand-caked hands. The next moment, they were filling the dump truck together because that's what kids can do, live so completely in the present moment, with no grudges carried over from the past.

Back on the swing again, I thought about our few rules at home that were nonnegotiable, providing us siblings with a sense of security because we knew where the behavior boundaries clearly lay. No hitting, biting, mean teasing, or screaming. Screaming got added after a group of my friends came over who insisted on screaming as we sprayed each other with the garden hose while playing on the grass.

Mom came out and let us have a piece of her mind, reminding us that hearing someone scream was almost heart-stopping. She solemnly told us that screaming should be designated to signify a real emergency, like a fire or serious accident. Watching my little brothers play together again, I was glad we had rules because it was never too early to learn to be respectful and responsible for our actions.

Then Bruce wanted the dump truck.

And Douglas...rolled it over to him.

And Bruce filled it with sand with his shovel, then rolled it back to Douglas, so he could dump the sand back out.

And with that, I headed into the house to bring the boys some snacks, because biting was fine for cookies.

Maintain clear behavior boundaries.

19.

Fuzzy Teeth

"SWEETIE, YOU CAN'T GO TO BED SWEATY WITH FUZZY teeth," said Dad.

"Sure I can," I countered.

"But you'll sleep so much better after a shower," he said.

"I'm asleep now," I said, slumping over my desk covered with homework, proving I couldn't possibly make it to the bathroom.

"C'mon, it only takes a minute," said Dad, which for him was true. He showered sometimes for only sixty seconds.

He'd grown up as a boy on an island in Canada and preferred sleeping in his tent down by the lake, away from the trauma of his home life. When it was too cold to bathe in Lake Ontario, he learned he could make a fire, boil a pot of lake water, funnel it into a special bag, hang the bag from a tree branch, and get a full minute of trickling hot water to shower. Or perhaps, sixty seconds was all the hot water he got during basic training in the Air Force during the Korean War. But whatever it was, every drop of water was precious to Pa.

But if you preferred to shower in the morning instead of at night, Dad would launch into his kayak trip story about how cooking dinner for his paddling buddies in time to watch the sunset, he'd forgotten to take his dip in the lake before sundown when the mosquitoes descended as big as biplanes. Poor Dad just couldn't fall asleep sweaty from paddling, and decided it was worth getting his butt bit racing to and from the lake in order to be squeaky clean for bedtime.

Thus, when we kids were small, we were bathed every night, and when we were older, we were responsible for our own cleanliness, which meant I got sent back to my room a few times to change out of my favorite clothes before trying to waltz out the door when I didn't smell as fresh as I should.

"Having healthy hygiene is just something we do," Dad said simply. "And if you shower tonight, I'll give you some Royalle Lyme," he offered.

That did it.

Dad never wore his favorite aftershave cologne anymore because he said it was too expensive. Shame. It was one of my favorite smells of childhood. One day, when I was around three or four years old, watching Dad shaving, suddenly I was lifted into the air, and placed standing on the bathroom counter. Then I got shaving cream on my face and proceeded to mimic Dad's every move in the mirror with my index finger. After we rinsed off the rest of the shaving cream, Dad took down from a shelf an olive-green glass bottle with a heavy lead lid shaped like a crown, poured a few precious drops into his hands, and patted them on my cheeks and then his.

Forever this smell is Dad.

Sixty seconds later, I was squeaky clean, having brushed my fuzzy teeth while showering in under a minute, rinse, lather, rinse—which I challenged Dad to time on his watch.

"You're going to sleep so much better," Dad said, kissing me goodnight on the forehead.

"I'm asleep now," I said, my eyes already closed, but I was smiling because tonight, I smelled like royal limes.

Have healthy personal hygiene.

20.

Little Kindnesses

THERE WAS A KNOCK ON MY BEDROOM DOOR. BUT NO one was in the hallway. Just a plate of cookies. Warm molasses spice. And a glass of milk.

I'm watching from the window: Iain cutting the grass, Douglas running across the lawn with a Popsicle, Iain pausing the ride-around mower sweating, accepting the melting Popsicle, Douglas now seated on Iain's lap steering, seven-year-old hands on the wheel with glee.

A plain cardboard box is transformed with magic markers, scissors, tape, and a mast by Iain, into a pirate ship for Bruce's Halloween costume, worn with suspenders.

A quiet day in the darkroom for Christopher gets cut short for Douglas's science project: drawing different designs, experimenting with liquid metal too hot to handle, until the small submarine submerged itself in the bathtub, amid celebratory shouts.

It's below freezing when I get outside to the driveway, but for some reason my car engine is already running. The windows free of ice with clues that Iain's new plastic driver's license makes a good scraper.

Late for a date but still showering, someone's shirt gets secretly ironed and laid out on their bed.

Iain sets up stones in the driveway to teach me how to parallel park, not cringing too much as I change gears, badly, in his car.

I don't remember Mom and Dad sitting us kids down to teach us to be thoughtful, starting with each other, so I guess we learned it through osmosis, because looking back, my childhood was laced with kindness. Looking for ways to help out was just one way to maintain balance in our busy household.

Still, if each thoughtful moment was a square, illustrated with needle and thread, it'd make a lovely quilt.

Practice being thoughtful.

21.

Knock-Knock

WHAM.

Iain slammed his bedroom door. He was mad.

Fine with me. But not really.

Somehow, Iain and I, sixteen and thirteen, had begun hurling insults back and forth in the hallway. Then I said something extra stinky, and he left, slamming his door. Then there was only silence while doing our homework, which is why I was sad.

At some point, a little game had gotten going where on school nights, Iain would knock on our shared wall, and I'd knock back. Then he'd wait a moment, knowing I was waiting for him to knock again, which always made me grin.

Finally, he'd knock again, and we'd go back to doing our homework.

Until he'd knock again. Sometime later.

But tonight, our wall was silent.

Then I remembered I had to wash my school uniform, so I went into the laundry room and stopped in my tracks. The center of the linen cabinet door was caved in, and there was a smudge of blood on the shattered wood.

Which smote my heart.

My carefully aimed verbal poisoned arrows had indeed reached their intended target—Iain's heart—and the negative energy had radiated outward.

Touching the splintered wood, I thought about the fact that the energy Iain used hitting the door was the same energy he used chopping firewood, baking his favorite pie, hitting a baseball, or lifting Douglas up on his shoulders for a better view.

But Life doesn't decide how we use its energy; we do.

We can use it to harm or hug, break or build, kick or kiss.

When I was about eleven, I asked Dad why Life didn't just *make* us be loving. He explained that we had to have free will because love couldn't be programmed in. Then it wouldn't be love. He said that we had to have the freedom to choose, for love to count.

I knocked on Iain's door. No answer.

Then I knockity-knocked, and he opened it.

He was cradling his right hand, but after a quick inspection, I saw only one knuckle was slightly grazed. My heart was bruised more.

"Really? A karate punch?" I said, trying to lighten the moment. He rolled his eyes, we each apologized, and we agreed we'd tell the parents that we'd been chasing each other for fun and run into the door.

Still, I had trouble falling asleep that night, since balance, once tipped over, takes its own time to reestablish itself. Finally, I got back out of bed and knocked on the wall. Iain waited before knocking back, knowing I was waiting. (Smile.) Then he knockity-knocked back, and I knew all was well.

Which made all the difference.

Fine with me.

Upset feelings have negative power.

22.

Wait Three Days

"I'M GONNA GET A WHAT?" I ALMOST YELLED INTO THE phone in my college dorm hallway, learning that Iain had had a little fender bender, but was absolutely fine. Now Mom said he was offering to fix up his old car for me, since he'd be getting a newer one for work.

"OK, calm down," Mom said. "It's not the pretti—"

"It's a car!" I interrupted, and my imagination took off at full speed picturing myself buying groceries off campus, toodling around the countryside, and going on picnics with my friends. "Mom, this is amazing. I've never had a car before."

"I know, dear," Mom said evenly. "But let's remember to wait the three days before telling anyone, OK?" And my imaginary ride slammed on its brakes.

Oh, right, the three-days thing. Forgot about that.

Mom and Dad had taught us that when we received some unexpected news—happy, sad, or bad—to wait three days before sharing it.

Why?

Well, for one thing, unexpected news can be emotionally charged, so waiting a bit before saying or doing anything about it allows your emotions to settle down and your thoughts to be more grounded.

Two, with your emotions settled, you see how you really feel beyond the surprise or shock of the moment, which is harder to recognize if you're leaping around the room or lying on the floor in a puddle.

Three, further implications of sudden news come more into focus when you're calm. The exception to the rule is a real emergency when you need immediate support, and then time is of the essence.

So, right after hanging up, instead of going back to my roommate, I headed down the hill for the covered bridge. That first day, I have to admit, every time I thought about the car, I was doing cartwheels in my head. Then I'd offer to let go of my feelings, pretending I was a sieve.

On day two, whenever I remembered, I just hummed silently to myself, and then got back to my studies. Calmer now, I began rehearsing different ways I could share the news so my friends would be happy, too, not sad they didn't have wheels. I was also grateful I hadn't blurted out on day one that they could borrow the car, only to learn that insurance wouldn't cover them and I'd have to take back my offer.

By day three, I was perfectly peaceful, and grateful Mom had reminded me to wait. Interesting that I had needed all three days.

As it turned out, it was nearly a month before Iain had the car fixed and could drive it up to me at Middlebury, so it was a good thing I hadn't been holding my breath.

"She's not much to look at," Iain said, affectionately patting the slightly rusty-in-quite-a-few-places olive-green Ford Pinto with fake wooden side panels. "But she's got a feisty engine and she'll get you from here to there. You might just have to lean forward when you go uphill a bit."

My friends and I gathered around her admiringly, one even jumping up and down now that we all had wheels. But I was feeling as calm as a cucumber, as peaceful as a…pickle, blessing Mom for my inner balance, a perfect state to be in behind the wheel.

Wait three days before sharing news.

23.

Talking like a Tennis Ball

ITALKTOOFAST.

I TALK TOO LOUD.

I talk tooooo much.

I even interrupt sometimes, which is incredibly rude because it gives the impression that I think what I'm saying is more important than what you're saying, even though I don't. Truly. I just get swept up in storytelling.

I also noticed recently that I have this way of talking right along with someone, filling in any spaces that might occur because they've paused for a moment to, you know, breathe.

I should whittle myself a talking stick.

Maybe find a lip balm in the flavor of superglue.

"Don't worry, sweetie," said Jenna, when I called her one day at work, forgetting to ask if I was interrupting. "You're a natural born storyteller. I love your stories."

"But...," I offered helpfully.

"But," she added, "if it's not a storytelling moment, girlfriend, you gotta pass the ball. Let the other person run with the conversation in their court a bit. No fun always watching the other guy dribble. A conversation should be more like a good tennis match; you know, back and forth."

"So, I'm a ball hog," I said flatly.

"I told you," she said, "I love how you turn everything into a story. But if you really want to start speaking less, perhaps think about why you feel the need to say all that you do." Which shut me up while obviously a new neural pathway was forming. "Also," she continued, "maybe silence isn't an empty space that needs to be filled." This also surprised the heck out of me because I'd never thought of it like that before.

"Now," she continued, "I've got three minutes before a meeting, but they're all yours." And I was just about to tell her a story of how I'd set a pigeon free that morning, whose wing had been caught in a plastic bag, bravely stopping traffic at a busy New York City intersection, and how when the bird flew away, cars, including taxis, honked happily and people cheered and waved, and what a cool little celebratory moment it had been.

But instead, I surprised myself and kept quiet.

"Nope, this is me practicing passing the ball, babe," I said. "It's in your court." And closed my mouth.

"In that case," Jenna said, "I think my new boss is bullying me." And went on with some examples.

"Yes, she is," I agreed after hearing her story. "And I can't believe you didn't call me sooner."

"I wasn't sure until I heard myself say it out loud," she said. "Now I need to think about what to do, so thank you for making a place for this issue to surface. Call you tonight."

And I sat for a moment in the silence afterward, aware in a new way that space, particularly in a conversation, isn't necessarily something that needs to be filled.

Speak thoughtfully.

24.

Sitting Smaller than Sunflowers

IT WAS A BEAUTIFUL SUNDAY AND, DRIVING THROUGH the Spanish countryside, Frédéric and I were admiring the expanse of blue and sky, with hardly an olive tree to break the horizon.

I was practicing speaking Spanish to him, and making mistakes every other word. He started shaking his head that he still had to correct every word and also in between, and he began laughing at me. Not with me. At least, that's how I interpreted the moment. And instead of rising to the occasion and laughing at myself, for some reason I'll never know, I chose to feel hurt.

But feelings are funny things. We don't ask them to come. Like clouds, they form from invisible vapors, but can swirl into something threatening in a heartbeat, no warning on the horizon.

Too bad. It was a very pretty Sunday.

And forgetting that I normally cared for peace more than protecting my personal point of view, I turned away and tears began to fall.

Frédéric playfully danced his hand over to my lap, no doubt to make amends, but thinking he was still making fun, my hand came down on top of his. *Slap!* He was so surprised at my overreaction, he started laughing again, and feeling that I wasn't getting through, I said, "Stop the car! I want to get out!"

He shook his head disbelievingly, but didn't slow down.

Now feeling rather powerless, I surprised myself and yelled, "Stop the car!"

Frédéric calmly pulled over.

The countryside was silent.

In strange slow motion, I removed my baseball cap, unbuckled my seat belt, opened the car door, and took off running. I ran up a small hill and straight into a sunflower field until I was out of sight.

Running through the dried sunflowers, suddenly, I felt very small. I had had no idea how much taller they were than I was, having never seen one in its entirety before. After a few moments, I slowed down and sat down on the powdery earth.

He doesn't understand, I thought, and I began to cry.

And Life...just let me sit there because they were my feelings. I could wallow in them as much as I liked. Eventually, my emotional storm passed, and I began listening to the absolute quiet all around me. Not a single bug buzzed. Looking up through the dried sunflowers towering over me, I saw patches of blue sky through their leaves and began to feel peaceful again.

My thought turned to my breath and slowly, I began more mindfully inhaling and exhaling...offering... *He doesn't understand* reappeared briefly in my thinking.

"It doesn't matter," Life revealed in my new inner quiet. "Your heart is always known."

Oh…?

Hmm…

I sat quietly with my new understanding for a few full breaths, feeling it in my center and allowing it to settle into my consciousness. Then I stood up, brushed the dirt from the back of my pants, and made my way through the sunflowers, more humble than before.

Frédéric was leaning up against the car, and as I approached, he opened his arms and folded me gently into them, saying, "Je suis désolé." (I'm sorry.)

"Moi aussi," I said into his chest. (Me too.)

"Tu es sensible." (You're sensitive.)

Happily, it was one of the reasons he chose me.

It was a beautiful Sunday, and driving through the countryside, Frédéric and I were admiring the expanse of blue and sky, and gazing at the fields of flowers spinning past, I found myself thanking them for their quiet patience and the wisdom I had found within.

Sitting smaller than sunflowers.

Remember that Life knows our hearts.

LIFE SKILL

#4. Letting Go

Builds Freedom

25.

Just You 'n' Me

I WAS SO WELL HIDDEN, THERE WAS NO WAY DAD WAS going to find me. Of course, he also wasn't going to look because that was our game. When he'd be leaving for a photography trip, I'd sneak out to the van and stow away. Then he'd start driving down our long driveway chuckling, and I'd start laughing, and before pulling out onto the main road, he'd stop, and I'd come out of my hiding place and hug him goodbye, because, of course, I never had the freedom to go because of school. But this time, Dad didn't stop.

"Wait, Daddy," I called, popping up from behind the camera cases. "I'm here."

"Well, then, c'mon out and buckle up 'cause we're goin' to Canada," he said, grinning into the rearview mirror.

"Just you 'n' me?" I asked incredulously.

"Just you 'n' me," he confirmed.

"What about school?" I asked, immediately sorry I'd blurted it out, lest he change his mind.

"Oh, Mom and I figured you could miss a few days. She called your teachers and got your homework." No way. I was goin' to

Canada. Then Dad made a U-turn in the neighbor's driveway, knowing I'd want to say a proper goodbye. Mom and my brothers were standing in the driveway grinning. My suitcase had already been packed.

I was appointed copilot, helping to read the map as we made our way from Ohio to Ontario and the Thousand Islands just north of the state of New York. Dad asked my opinion about everything: when we should stop, where to eat, and whether to take a fast route or a prettier road that was a bit longer. I suddenly felt more grown up than I really was, and maybe he got to relax a bit as a dad as we junk-fooded our way across several state lines.

The scenery got prettier with every passing hour, and we sang along to cassettes Dad had made of Neil Young. But the best part of the trip was having all of Dad's attention for myself. He told me stories of growing up on Wolfe Island, skipping over the sadder parts of his unaffectionate father who could be violent and unpredictable when drunk. During this trip, he only shared the fun parts of his childhood, like learning to drive a pickup truck at fourteen...zipping across the lake to Kingston in a motorboat to get fresh bait and supplies for his father's fishing inn on the island...sneaking with some buddies into a neighbor's field to eat watermelon by moonlight.

He told me how the next summer as a new teenager, he began working diligently for this same kind farmer, picking whatever crops were ripe for three cents a box, sometimes wishing he was swimming or fishing with his friends instead of sweating in the summer sun working, but still glad to be earning some spending money.

For the first time, I saw Dad at my age of fourteen, already preferring to sleep outdoors in his tent under the starry sky, where he could hear the lake lapping on its rocky shore, his brown-and-white dog, Colonel, some friendly company.

I didn't know then that it'd be the only trip I ever took alone with Dad before I left home for good, and because of that, whenever he and Mom came to visit me in Europe, I always planned a little alone time with each of them.

Alone with each of them was never the same as being the three of us together.

I tested this theory, once, going for a walk with Mom, where we animatedly talked the whole time about interesting things. I did the same walk alone with Dad the next day, and we, too, talked about meaningful things the whole time. But the next morning, all three of us went for a walk, and the most profound exchange after quite a bit of silence was, "These leaves sure are crunchy," so go figure.

As Dad and I drove off the ferry crossing to Canada, the sun was just setting, and we headed straight for his favorite place for dinner. The fried fish 'n' chips were sizzling hot and wrapped in newspaper the way he always remembered, and it was one of the yummiest memories of my life so far. Not just because the fish had probably been swimming that afternoon in Lake Ontario, but because all day long, I'd had all of Dad's attention, and he'd had all of mine.

What freedom just being two.

And it was only day one.

Just Dad 'n' me.

Sometimes make a memory for just two.

26.

I Trust Me

"WHAT ABOUT *ALIEN*?" PROPOSED DAD ONE SUMMER evening while we were looking at the newspaper to see what movies were playing.

"I'm happy to go," said Christopher.

"Me too," Iain chimed in.

"I don't think it's a film for me," said Mom. "I'll stay home with the little boys so you guys can go." Moms. Then I took a deep breath.

"I'd like to go," I ventured. "It looks like fun."

"Honey," Mom began, "it looks really scary. Besides, it's rated R."

"But Mom," I said, acutely aware I had a better chance of sounding more mature if I spoke thoughtfully, rather than emotionally. "R is for seventeen and older. I'm seventeen now. If it gets too scary, I'll just close my eyes. Besides," I added, looking at Dad for support, "Dad'll be there."

Mom and Dad exchanged glances, having a pact to have a united front so we kids didn't try to divide and conquer, which on occasion worked. They also understood that once you see something, you can't unsee it, which is why they were careful choosing what our young, impressionable minds got exposed to.

"I won't have nightmares, trust me," I said, knowing full well that I never watched horror movies exactly for this reason. Finally, seeing it was OK with Dad, Mom gave in, although she seemed sad when I hugged her goodbye.

But just before we reached the end of our driveway, I asked Dad to stop the car. "I'm not sure I should go," I said, feeling torn not having Mom's approval but wanting to go. "I think I'm old enough to decide for myself, but I feel bad doing something Mom thinks I shouldn't do."

I remember Dad turning to me and saying something to the effect that parenting was about getting me ready to be safely on my own in the world, which began with learning how to make my own decisions. Dad said he thought I was old enough, but that Mom was more sensitive about these things. But if I felt that I could trust myself, I could help Mom see that she could too.

"OK," I said, making up my mind and feeling peaceful with my decision. "Let's go." And off we went.

I had a great time, despite having to remind myself that I was watching actors in costumes, and that there were people just off camera in jeans and T-shirts holding microphones during the scariest parts.

Still, that night, I hoped I could skip dreams about aliens, and replayed scenes of Bambi and Thumper going for a walk with Mom in my head until I fell asleep.

Luckily, in the morning, I awoke serenely with no memory of scary dreams. At breakfast, I decided not to tell Mom about the kitchen table scene that had shocked me so much I'd grabbed Dad's arm, who, in letting out an involuntary yell, made the audience around us laugh, and just stuck to the fun parts.

"Thanks for trusting me," I said, hugging her.

"So, moms can be wrong," she said, hugging me back. "I guess you're ready to decide for yourself now," she added, which I really appreciated, realizing that it mustn't be easy for parents to let go so kids have the freedom to make decisions on their own.

Still, I'm grateful for the conscious monitoring Mom and Dad did when I was young, aware that even now, we cannot unsee something we've seen, so it's worth taking care choosing what plays on the big screen of our minds.

Monitor what you watch.

27.

Superhero

I WAS WATCHING HER. CLOSELY.

I don't think parents know that.

That we kids are watching them, and that they're teaching us how to be. One way or another.

But mostly I'd started watching Mom because recently, I had a sneaky suspicion that she was a superhero and I hoped that I'd catch her changing, you know, into her cape and boots.

The other morning, for example, she passed me with the vacuum cleaner going one way, only to have a garden hoe in her hands a few moments later, and when I turned around to mention this, she was walking in the front door with groceries, when I could've sworn I had just passed her in the hallway carrying a basket of freshly folded laundry.

Then when I went downstairs to the studio, there was Mom in her office editing a script with a pencil in one hand, and adding figures on a calculator with the other, not even looking at the keypad. I was just about to ask if she could kindly make me a dentist appointment, when she looked up and she told me that I already had one, even though I hadn't asked for it yet.

Then going back upstairs, I looked out the window and saw Mom lugging two pails of water out to the fruit trees we'd planted the day before, since the hose didn't reach. But by the time I got my tennis shoes on to help her, she was washing the car in the driveway.

See what I mean?

Mom was everywhere, taking care of everything.

All at once.

Only superheroes do that.

But there's more.

Mom was flowing merrily along, not bumping and grumping, but moving mindfully with a quiet smile in her eyes.

That's when a little explosion went off in my head.

I didn't have to be afraid that Mom was turning fifty. Age was just a number! Look at her! With every trip around the sun, Mom seemed more amazing, more patient, more wise, and my concept of aging shattered the way preconceived notions do when confronted with reality. In fact, to my eighteen-year-old eyes, Mom was getting even *cooler* with every passing year.

I still haven't seen Mom change into her cape yet, but I did catch her lacing up her hiking boots so she could climb to the top of the still-steaming manure mountain she requested for her birthday from the farm down the road. Poised with my pitchfork to help put the fresh fertilizer on her flower garden, I couldn't stop watching her.

Even on her birthday, Mom's only mission was to help things *grow*.

See what I mean?

Only a superhero does that.

Celebrate the wisdom of each new year.

28.

Wonder Twins

"HEY, WONDER TWIN, WANNA GO DANCING?" ASKED Iain one Friday night. It was 1981, and he was home from college for spring break during my senior year of high school.

"Dancing?" I asked, surprised. "Are you kidding? I'd love to."

Zooming along the freeway, Iain turned down the radio that we'd been singing to and became uncharacteristically serious. "So, I need to tell you something. The place we're going to is a gay bar. Is that OK with you?"

"Sure," I said, having no idea what he meant.

"That means there's mostly only guys there. You'll be one of the few girls."

"I don't care," I said, absolutely not caring. "It's Friday night. I'm with you and we're going dancing downtown." And I was grinning, which made him visibly relax and turn the radio back up.

Once inside the club, I thought I was in *Saturday Night Fever*. There were silver disco balls hanging from the ceiling, swiveling colored lights, and laser beams shooting across the dance floor.

It was nearly empty, so we headed for the bar when suddenly, we heard, "Girlfriend!" and a small herd of multihued boys came galloping across the dance floor straight for Iain. (I later learned that he—karate team captain, cabinetmaker, mechanic, and race-car driver—hated being called "girlfriend," which, of course, was why they called him that.) I watched in wonder as they hugged him with genuine affection, kissing him on each cheek the way they do in Europe, two boys giving him a quick peck on the lips.

"Guys," Iain said blushing, "I'd like to intro—"

"Oh, girl, you got a twin!" said his friend from Jamaica.

"You two are identical!" added his friend from Venezuela. "She's just got more hair!"

"It's Donnie and Marie!" said his Swedish friend, grinning.

"Honored to meet you, honey," said his Filipino friend. "I love your shoes." Whereupon everyone looked down at my flats and said how lovely I looked and asked me to twirl in my miniskirt, which I did. I'd never experienced anything like it before: instant unconditional acceptance from some of the most interesting and loving people I had ever met.

Then Earth, Wind & Fire's "September" started to play, and the rest of the night was a deafening, joyous blur as we basically danced nonstop until we closed the place down. I don't think I ever stopped smiling.

Later, as we pulled out of the parking lot, Iain asked if I was hungry, which I was, and while eating the Early Bird Special of two eggs, two strips of bacon, two sausages, and two pancakes each at a nearby diner, Iain told me his story as the sun began to rise.

It was not an easy road for Iain, being raised in a family in 1970s Ohio, and coming out as openly gay in a time and place when our society was just beginning to start the hard work of recognizing and respecting the dignity of those they deemed "different." And just a few short years later, that difficulty was compounded and overshadowed as we began to lose friends and family to the tragedy of HIV while so many chose to avert their eyes instead of working toward meaningful treatment.

Mom and Dad found it challenging to choose full acceptance over adherence to the social and spiritual beliefs they had been taught, but Iain was patient and steadfast that he had the right to live and love openly, and he slowly won over our parents.

One of Iain's friends described him at his college graduation as the kind of person who gets up early in the morning to put baby birds back in their nests, which seemed accurate to me.

To this day, I treasure all the dancing I've done with Iain in gay bars. I believe that the unconditional love, respect, and acceptance that I received during my own formative years from friends in what is now called the LGBTQ+ community helped me suspend judgment and is a cornerstone of my friendships, emotional health, and well-being.

And I'm forever grateful for that.

So, bless you, Iain, for taking me out and coming out to me that special spring night and for sharing with me your truest, most complete self. I wouldn't have you any other way, and I love that people seeing our close bond and family resemblance still wonder aloud if we are twins. Please know that you'll always have a dancing partner in me.

Respect every soul.

29.

A Moose on the Dunes

"HEY, YOU, TGIF!" SAID MOOSIE. "WATCHA DOING?"

"Traveling through Europe," I said, looking at a map on my desk. Six years older than Bruce, I'd already graduated from college, but after interning for a psychologist and working in a mental health hospital, a shelter for teenagers, a prison, and assisting support sessions for eating disorders, depression, and self-harm, I was no closer to discovering my life's passion or purpose. In fact, I had started feeling depressed myself, unsure if I was being helpful in any way.

Seeing me flounder, Mom and Dad offered me the chance to come home for a while and hired me so I wouldn't fall behind on my student loan payments until I figured out the next chapter of my life.

Still, it was Friday afternoon.

"Wanna go somewhere?" Bruce asked.

"Sure," I said.

"The sand dunes?" he said.

"Minnesota has sand dunes?" I asked, looking up.

"Nope," he said, galloping into my room and placing an atlas on top of my map of Europe. "But Colorado does. I planned the whole trip driving Douglas home from school just now, but he doesn't want to go."

"For how long?" I asked, seeing he was serious.

"Well, it takes a day to get there and a day back," he said. "So let's say four days, tops."

"When do you want to leave?" I asked.

He looked at his watch.

"And just think," he said, his eyes positively twinkling, "we can talk the whole way." Which touched me.

Several hours later, we were driving out the driveway. Mom and Dad thought it was a great idea, and Dad already had everything anyone could ever need to go camping labeled in boxes in the garage, bless his heart.

That's how fast you can turn on a dime sometimes if you have the freedom, provided that balance is already part of the picture. I also believe that Mom and Dad thought driving for a few days under so much big sky might be conducive to Bruce's and my brainstorming together. We were each at a point in our lives where we needed to think about what possible futures lay upon the horizon.

We talked nonstop the whole way. And back.

We stopped only for gas, ice cream, and photographs. We shared our thoughts, dreams, fears, regrets, concerns about the present, and hopes for the future, imagining out loud different scenarios for ourselves.

We woke just before dawn at Colorado's National Sand Dunes Park, making the first footprints of the morning on the smooth mountains of sand the night's wind had swept clean. I'll never forget how one side became gold as the sun rose, and the other side remained deep purple in the shadows, and how you could walk along the top with a foot in each color, warm sand and freezing cold.

Four and a half days later, we were back home, but not the same.

Our thoughts had…stretched.

A week later, Bruce found me again poring over a colorful map of Europe.

"TGIF," he said. "Wanna go somewhere?"

"I do," I said, looking up. "I think I want to go to Europe."

"I was thinking more like ice cream," he said.

"When do you want to go?" I asked.

He looked at his watch.

I followed him out the door, and this time, Douglas wanted to come.

Sometimes be spontaneous.

30.

The Runaway Guitar

ONE SUNNY FRIDAY, I DROVE DOWN FROM COLLEGE TO the Big Apple to spend Easter weekend with Iain. He lived on a lovely block on the Upper West Side where horses clip-clopped to the park from a riding school, and music filled the air from a Hispanic ballet studio, so it sounded like *West Side Story* when their windows were open.

We were unloading my car, carrying my things up three flights of stairs, but when I went back down to get my guitar, the car was empty. Puzzled, I looked up the sidewalk and saw a guy carrying what looked like my guitar case.

"Iain," I said, pointing, "I think that guy just stole my guitar!"

"Hey," Iain yelled in the guy's direction, and to our great surprise, the guy took off running and disappeared around the corner with my guitar.

I couldn't believe it.

"You go that way, and I'll go this way," Iain directed and away we went, because one, it was broad daylight so it didn't seem too scary, and two, we were in pretty good shape, and three, it was my beloved guitar.

Around the corner I raced and saw the guy moving as fast as one could while carrying a guitar. I began closing in fast, though I wasn't sure what I'd do once I caught up, because he was a lot bigger than I was.

Meanwhile, Iain appeared from the other direction and was now in front of the guy, who seemed surprised to find himself flanked. Suddenly, he propped my guitar against a parked car, crossed the street, and started sauntering away.

Then he yelled over his shoulder, "It's not mine," holding up his empty hands as if to prove that the guitar had run around the block by itself.

"You're right," Iain yelled back in a voice that sounded way too happy, and I just stood there with my mouth hanging open, partly from the audacity of the guy, and partly because I was still panting from my fun little run.

But suddenly, I was mad.

I could feel a wave of negatively charged atoms begin to gather from my emotional depths, gaining silent speed, a wave of pure potential carrying with it the power to—

To do what, exactly? interrupted my inner voice with such clarity I stopped, startled. *Blow up the world?* I snapped to attention, astonished my higher consciousness would call me out for just feeling upset. I hadn't done anything. Yet. *What happened to our fork in the road?*

Oh, right. That.

I'd designed a simple mental mnemonic, a signpost with two signs pointing in the opposite direction at a fork on a very picturesque country road, to help me through upsetting moments.

One said THIS WAY. The other said THAT WAY.

The signs changed depending upon the situation. LOVING–UNLOVING. PATIENT–IMPATIENT. To remind me to consciously choose which way to go.

I'd come up with the exercise after losing it with Mom once, saying something disrespectful that I sincerely regretted later. But no Control/Z really undoes an unkind moment, even if we're forgiven. We cannot undo spiteful words once said.

Then I noticed that Iain was doing a formal waltz with my guitar case.

"Are you dancing on the sidewalk with my guitar?" I asked.

"I am," Iain said. "It's Friday, you're here, and we got your guitar back. Let's celebrate. Let's *really* go dancing."

Disarmed by his joy, it took me only a moment to choose LET GO instead of HOLD ON at the fork in the road, and the wave of upset emotions that had been gathering dissolved like sea foam instead.

What a wild process the transformation of negative energy into positive must look like at the subatomic level. But at least I knew what it looked like on a sidewalk in New York City that day, which was Iain and me dancing with my guitar all the way home.

Choose your feelings.

31.

Once Seventeen

A WARM WIND WHIRRED SOFTLY THROUGH THE summer leaves and the sky was a heron's gray blue. It was the perfect sound for sleeping. I was on my way for a siesta when my maternal grandfather walked into the kitchen, having just awakened from his.

My visit from Spain happened to overlap with my grandparents' this time. They came to see Mom and Dad once a year in Minnesota, driving all the way from Arizona. Although I was still jet-lagged, something told me to take this time alone with Granddaddy, as it might never come again.

It never did.

I invited him outside onto the wooden deck to look out over the lake, and it didn't take long for him to begin storytelling, and the lake fell away for me.

Howard had grown up in Washington, DC, the eldest of four boys. His mother was an immigrant from Germany, and his father worked at the post office. The summer he was fourteen, he went to the countryside to work on a farm. There he built up the muscles on his skinny frame milking cows, pitching hay, planting, and picking crops.

One evening, while the farmer was away, the farmer's wife decided to burn a hornets' nest off the corner of their farmhouse. But suddenly, a breeze came up, catching the roof on fire, and the whole farmhouse burned to the ground. Howard had to leap from his bedroom to the ground, forgetting his two shirts and pairs of pants on the back of a chair, which was all he had. The tragedy was heartbreaking, because even young Howard knew it could've been prevented.

When he was seventeen, a friend invited him to a church social, where he saw my grandmother Claire for the first time. Afterward, he made sure he was the one walking home next to her, and he told his friend that night, "I've found the girl for me." About to celebrate sixty-one years of marriage, I smiled knowing that he had.

He told me how he was the first one in his family to attend college, working a full-time day job to go to school at night for eight years to earn a degree in engineering. When he was offered a job as a metallurgist in Ohio, he proposed to my grandmother with a telegram that said, "Got a job in Columbus. Will you come?"

He told me how lucky he felt doing experiments with metal alloys for jet airplanes and how during World War II, his work was so top secret, he was kept stateside. But after the war was over, his work sent him to England. He was scheduled to fly on to France, but something delayed his trip for one day. The next morning, while waiting for his breakfast in a London hotel, a friend solemnly placed a newspaper on Granddaddy's breakfast plate. The headline announced that the plane he would have been on had crashed in the English Channel and all aboard had been killed.

"So I wouldn't be here," I said, placing my hand on his arm, "if you had taken that flight."

"That's right," he said, patting my hand.

Still, the story of his flight home was adventurous enough. He described how when their small plane was approaching Newfoundland, the airfield had completely disappeared under a blanket of fog. The pilot was forced to keep circling, having aborted several landing attempts already. Only when they were nearly out of gas did a small hole appear in the clouds below, and they made a quick dive through it to land safely, with fire trucks waiting nearby. Granddaddy said he nearly kissed the ground that day.

Later, when Granny awoke, she joined his storytelling, and I only regret that I didn't record them to capture the sound of their voices and the little details I'll forget one day.

Until that afternoon, I had never thought about my grandparents looking differently than they did, even though I'd seen photographs. Of course, they, too, once had dark hair, strong muscles, supple bodies, and cheeks flushed with passion. Looking at them holding hands that afternoon, I realized that they had the privilege of being wise because they had the privilege of growing older.

It was the last time I saw Granddaddy conscious, and the last thing he said was, "I love you and I'll be at your upcoming wedding, one way or another."

I believe he was, somewhere wafting around the chandeliers as we danced, for he passed over the rainbow a few months before.

It was a great honor to know him, and after listening to his life stories that afternoon on the lake, I began looking at others in their golden years with a new kind of reverence and respect. Every one of them is a reservoir of wonder and wisdom. Every one of them has a life story to tell, as each and every one was once seventeen.

Ask elders for their stories.

32.

Pink Pauses

IT WAS A BEAUTIFUL SUNNY DAY, AND I FELT LIKE HUGging…everyone.

Just before walking out the door to head across Central Park, I stopped and did my few-minute morning meditation, ending with a pledge to be thoughtful the whole day long. It was something Mom and Dad had taught us to do when we were small before leaving for school, so we had a principle to back up against if we found ourselves getting into unkind thoughts.

But no sooner did I walk out the door when stimuli from the world around me began bombarding my senses and my brain began churning out thoughts.

They went something like this:

What a beautiful day. Oh, look, a baby. Looks like a newborn. Happy mama. Oh, the flowers are coming out. Whatta cute car. Wish I had a car like that. Look at Grandma 'n' Grandpa. Holding hands. Hope that's me one day. That's a pretty girl. Pretty dress. Wonder where she bought that? Wild hair. Ugly purse. Would never put those shoes with that dress. Wow, he's tall. What big sunglasses. That's a lotta tattoos. Does everyone have tattoos now? You'd think—

and then the street light changed and we pedestrians suddenly came to a group halt.

What. Are. You. Doing? demanded my higher self. *Opinions, opinions, opinions. Excuse me, but exactly who appointed you judge? How many times have I told you that personal opinions don't hold water? What happened to your pledge?* I looked around to see if anyone else could hear her, because she was being extra loud today.

But no one else seemed to hear anything.

Oh, and guess what? she continued, putting her hands on her hips, *Every sniff, snort, and sneer you're forming? Gets stored someplace. In your soul. Which means you get to carry 'em around. And there they'll stay, takin' up space, unless you offer to let them go.* Then the light changed, and we all began crossing the street to the park.

I needed a moment.

I made a hard right and headed for the nearest park bench.

I needed a pink pause.

Stop signs are red.

My pause signs are pink.

I found the first empty bench, sat down, and leaned over, plucking a nearby dandelion with all the wishes still intact.

I slowly inhaled and exhaled one full breath. Then another.

Well, you know my heart, I began. *It's not my intention to form opinions like these, much less hold onto them.* And I sat there, silently offering.

And in my stillness, although all the noise of the busy world was buzzing around me, a tiny message surfaced.

Just be kind.

Why, of course.

And I blew on the dandelion...

And with that, I was back on track.

It was a beautiful sunny day, and looking out with kind eyes, I got the sense that we're all doing the best we can. And I felt like hugging...everyone.

Just be kind.

LIFE SKILL

#5. Being Loving & Respectful

Builds Kindness

33.

Toads and Diamonds

"ARE THOSE TOADS OR DIAMONDS FALLING FROM YOUR mouth?" Mom called up the stairs one afternoon, and I froze midsentence. I hung my twelve-year-old head over the banister and held my breath. Mom stood gazing up at me.

"Gently, sweetheart," she said. "They're little. They're learning. And you," she added, "are teaching them." And that was that. No scolding. No lecture. She knew I understood. It was from one of my favorite fairy tales when I was small.

I'd been speaking like a witch.

I'd been scolding my little brothers for having both clean and dirty clothes mixed together with books and toys all over their bedroom floor. Days before, I'd spent half a day deep-cleaning and organizing all their stuff in the closet, as much a gift to them as a surprise for Mom. Yet I knew that using an upset voice could upset others around me. It was all about vibrations.

Emotions can speak louder than words.

In the fairy tale "Toads and Diamonds," two stepsisters are drawing water from a well when an old woman asks for a drink. One sister turns her away speaking harshly, whereas the other sister speaks kindly and patiently gives her a drink. The old woman, an enchantress in disguise, casts a silent spell upon them as they leave. When the sister with the selfish, hard heart later speaks at home, snakes and toads fall from her mouth. When the sister with the open, loving heart speaks, diamonds and pearls fall from her lips.

You can imagine who got the prince.

The moral of this cautionary tale is simple: intention and tone matter.

In fact, how we say something is often the real message.

In case I needed any proof, only minutes later I heard Bruce and Douglas heatedly blaming each other for the mess, when before, they'd been playing happily together in the mess they'd both made. It reminded me that children act by example, and having heard me speaking to them like a shrew, they had quickly adopted the same tone with each other.

When I came into their bedroom, Bruce and Douglas ran and hid themselves behind their curtains. I dropped to my knees to be their size, apologizing for using my witchy voice. They both threw their arms around me, happy that whatever evil spell had been cast upon their big sister was now broken.

Then together we began tidying their room again because they were little. They were learning. And I was teaching them.

Tone speaks louder than words.

34.

Carrots Don't Hop

IT WAS A QUIET EVENING DURING THE SUMMER, AND the seven of us had just finished dinner. I was already back in my bedroom and, walking by my mirror, I caught my eleven-year-old reflection and found myself saying, "You know what? That was a really good dinner, and I didn't even say, 'Thank you' to Mom." Then I imagined myself going back to say it, which seemed silly now that dinner was over, but having imagined it, it seemed right to go.

The sun was setting, backlighting Mom through the kitchen window, where I found her quietly washing the pots and pans. She always volunteered to do them while the rest of us cleared the table, loaded the dishwasher, and wiped the counters after a meal.

Watching her, it struck me how alone she looked with only the humming of the dishwasher to keep her company. This was the reason we kids didn't like doing the pots and pans: they always took longer than the rest of the kitchen, and no one wanted to be alone at the end. It had never occurred to me that maybe she didn't prefer it either.

"Oh," I said, coming into the kitchen, "you're all alone."

"Oh," she replied, shrugging her shoulders, "I don't mind. I always have something to think about."

"Mom," I began, "I was thinking about how yummy the dinner was, the roast chicken, the carrots, the mashed potatoes and gravy, and I realized that I didn't say 'Thank you,' so, thank you for the lovely dinner."

"You're welcome," she said absentmindedly, picking up a greasy oven tray to scrub, but I could tell she wasn't really listening.

"No, Mom, I mean it," I said, starting to pace. "When I think about all the meals you and Dad have cooked all these years, I can't believe I never thought of saying, 'Thank you.'"

I stopped and placed my hand on her arm so she'd stop scrubbing for a moment and listen. "So, I want to thank you for them all now." Mom sighed a deep sigh but smiled, rinsed the suds off the last pot, and put it upside down on the counter, and then she looked at me.

"Well," she said, drying her hands on a tea towel, "I appreciate that. Making a meal takes time. It takes energy and thought. Potatoes don't peel themselves. Carrots don't hop into the pot on their own. Someone's hands have been busy. So, thank you for being appreciative." And she leaned over, kissed me on the top of my head, hung up the damp tea towel, and walked out of the kitchen.

But I lingered a bit longer, watching the fading shadows of the tree branches dance upon the counter's surface in the evening breeze. I was proud of my small decision to begin a new pattern of thanking whoever made my meals.

Then I picked up the dish towel and dried the pots and pans that Mom had left to drip dry and put them away one by one, knowing that pots and pans don't hop off the counter and into the cupboard on their own.

Appreciate someone else's cooking.

35.

A Most Gracious Guest

THE SUMMER I WAS FOURTEEN, A FRIEND INVITED ME to visit her in Maine during summer vacation. It was one of my first times away from home, and before I left, Mom sat with me while I was packing to remind me what it meant to be a gracious guest.

"Always keep your things tidy," she began, counting out my socks, "meaning no clothes on the floor, even if they're dirty. That's just being polite in someone's else's home."

"Keep my things tidy," I repeated, folding a sundress.

"Make your bed first thing in the morning," she said next. "It makes a difference to the whole state of your room."

"Make my bed," I said, tucking in a bathing suit and flip-flops. "Wait, I always make my bed," I added, and Mom nodded, not listening.

"Leave the bathroom clean, if not cleaner that you found it," she continued, handing me my T-shirts. "That includes checking the shower drain, sink, and floor. No one else needs to clean up your pretty hair."

"Deal," I said, nodding, having found enough on the bathroom floor once to make a small rug.

"Remember to ask, 'What can I do to help?' especially around mealtime. Offer to set the table. Nip the beans. Slice the strawberries. Wash the lettuce. Pluck the chicken. Catch the fish. Insist if they politely refuse. Tell them you're leaving if they don't give you something to do."

"Got it," I said. "You know that I know these things already, don't you, Mom?" I asked, tilting my head sideways.

"I know you know, dear," she said, smiling. "I'm just being a mom, reminding you. Oh, one more thing. Take a hostess gift. I have some homemade raspberry jam, unless you have another idea."

"Homemade jam's perfect," I said.

"Finally," she concluded, handing me my shorts, "it's up to you to remember to write a thank-you note soon after your stay. I'm only mentioning it now in case you want to write it while you'll still there and leave it for them to discover after you've gone. If you remember these little things, you'll be a very welcome guest. I'd be happy to have you anytime."

"I'll remember," I said, zipping my suitcase closed.

As it turned out, it was one of the most memorable summers of my life. It began with my first airplane ride to Boston. Then we drove up the coast, my girlfriend's mother reading *The Hobbit* out loud along the way.

I'd never stayed near an ocean before, and I was in awe of how the water in the bay was deep enough to swim in during the late afternoon, but gave way to shiny mudflats I could walk on in the early morning, as far as I could see.

Over just those few weeks, I experienced my first crush, fell in love with maple butter, dug for clams, picked wild blueberries, played my first softball game, got up on water skis for almost a full moment, and saw turquoise phosphorous illuminating the crests of waves as they crashed to shore one night.

Dutifully asking, "What can I do to help?" daily, I ended up doing my fair share of setting the table, washing the dishes, and scrubbing pots and pans. I pitched in with Saturday chores of vacuuming, dusting, and bathroom cleaning, even offering to mop the kitchen floor on my own. I truly felt like a member of the family. Not a guest. Which was the best part of all.

On my last day, listening at the bay window and trying to memorize the sound of the waves, I wrote a thank-you card from a set I'd found on my bed as a welcome gift, describing all the new experiences the family had given me and how much it had meant.

I left it on my pillow for them to find after I left.

It must have really touched them, because I got a thank-you letter from the mother, thanking me for my thank-you letter. And one more thing, which Mom said was the best compliment ever.

An invitation back.

Be a gracious guest.

36.

The Midnight Message

EVERYONE WAS SOUND ASLEEP WHEN I ARRIVED HOME around midnight, so I was extra quiet going down the stairs to my bedroom. I was visiting Mom and Dad during a break from graduate school, with the added joy of seeing my grandmother, who was now living with them since Granddaddy had passed the spring before. Hearing the wind pick up, I knew I was going to sleep well. A lullaby of leaves. There were no trees outside my bedroom window in New York City.

I was in the bathroom brushing my teeth by the soft glow of a nightlight, when, looking in the mirror, I remembered that Mom had asked me to make Granny her snack whenever I arrived home. Sometimes she just needed a little something to tide her over till morning.

But I'm so tired, I thought, making a face in the mirror. *Maybe she won't miss it this one night*. But imagining Granny waking up and not finding anything, I knew I had to go. Plus, I'd promised Mom. So back up the stairs I went.

Tiptoeing around, I made some toast, buttered it, cut it up

into bite-sized squares, plopped them into a mug of milk, added a sprinkle of sugar, and heated it in the microwave.

I carried the hot mug carefully down the stairs, snuck noiselessly into Granny's bedroom, and was feeling around for her night table in the dark, when I heard a giggle.

"Is that you?" asked Granny.

"No," I said, giggling back. "What are you doing awake, young lady?" I turned on a low light and sat down on her bed. Granny was all smiles.

"I haven't been asleep yet," she confessed. "But I've been having such fun hearing you pad around outside my door. It just sounded so friendly." My heart skipped a beat.

Knowing she was happier with company, I snuggled up close while she ate her snack. I thought about how things had gone around...how now it was grown up me tucking in my grandmother...when it used to be Granny tucking in a tiny me. Then I kissed her goodnight and made a beeline for the bathroom.

"Thank you, thank you, thank you," I whispered earnestly to my reflection. "Imagine not choosing to have brought her milk." And I thought of her hearing all my going to bed noises, then my bedroom door opening and closing, and silence.

No snack for Granny.

And that's when I got a midnight message.

It would've been rather startling if it hadn't been so gently revealed.

That's all that's needed...this one thing...
for you to be your most loving self.

My actions had been...*witnessed*.

I stood there pondering this revelation for a long while... looking into my own eyes in the mirror...reflecting on the idea that all is known…every act of kindness…or the withholding thereof.

Life is watching.

Then I yawned.

It was a lot for my sleepy head.

Later, listening to the wind as my eyelids grew heavy, I felt deeply grateful for the inner message that all seems known somehow…somewhere…in the Universe.

In fact, it felt very comforting, feeling that I was forever being watched.

And Life added, in its silent way of revealing inner things,

Watched *over*.

⚜

Be your most loving self.

37.

Magic Hugs

HUGS ARE FILLED WITH MAGIC.

Truly.

One heartfelt hug can re-center you. Congratulate you. Soothe ruffled feathers. Ease physical pain. Help heal. Remind you how insanely important you are.

So important, in fact, that someone wants to share the same square feet of the earth's surface that you're occupying and wrap their arms around you.

But that summer day when Douglas was eight, he didn't want a hug when I offered him one. He just picked up his suitcase and walked out the door.

"Mom," I called, watching him plod away, "I think Douglas just ran away from home." Mom joined me at the window, and we watched him resting his suitcase every few steps going down the driveway. Probably books. We tried not to smile.

"He'll be back when he's ready," Mom said reassuringly.

"Or eaten all his snacks," Dad called from the kitchen, also watching from the window. Then they both went nonchalantly back to work in the studio.

I loved moments like these when I could just breathe easy knowing that Mom and Dad were at the helm, taking care of things. As responsible as I felt being a big sister, finally, they were the parents. I could relax. Plus, they had this uncanny way of knowing when to hold the line, having set a limit, and when flexibility was key. But most of all, I knew Douglas would come back because Mom and Dad had worked really hard to create a home where we kids felt safe, loved, and absolutely wanted. And best of all, they reinforced this daily.

With hugs.

Interestingly enough, neither Mom nor Dad were raised with a lot of hugs, so it's good to know you don't have to have had a warm 'n' fuzzy role model to do things differently when raising little people. And even though I believe a huge percentage of my well-being comes from having been hugged from a toddler to a teen, Frédéric wasn't hugged growing up either, and he turned out fine. So I guess it's knowing how much you're loved that really counts.

A few hours later, Douglas opened the front door, plopped his suitcase down, and said simply, "I'll take that hug now."

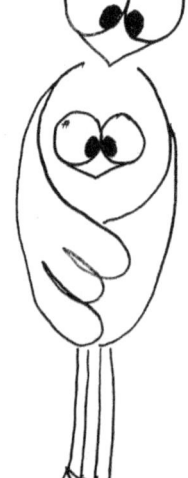

Without missing a beat, my fourteen-year-old arms went around him, expressing a myriad of messages all at once.

I care. You're not alone. I'm here.

But perhaps as you're standing heart-to-heart on the same tiny bit of the earth's surface that another is occupying that moment, what a hug really says is, "I'm so glad *you're* here."

See what I mean?

Hugs are filled with magic.

Hugs are filled with magic.

38.

Oh, It Was Nothing

"SO, I HEARD FROM MOM THAT YOU AND DOUGLAS swapped cars again," I said to Iain over the phone one Saturday morning. "Just can't get rid o' that thing, can you?" I added mischievously. He'd sold his car after a few years to Christopher, who after driving it a few more years, then sold it to Douglas. Douglas was now trading it back to Iain for Iain's newer car plus cash, since Iain could fix anything under a hood, and Douglas still didn't know how to open one. Iain just hadn't expected his old car to break down ten minutes after Douglas zoomed merrily away.

"Ha ha," Iain said, unamused. "So there I was, on the side of the road, searching for the emergency tool kit I was pretty sure was no longer in the car, when the hatchback door crashes down on my head, because gee, Douglas forgot to tell me that the strut was broken. Then it starts to rain, and while a lump's forming on my head, my backside's getting soaked."

"Poor you," I said, trying to hide the grin in my voice.

"So I missed my dinner, my movie date, and instead got four fun-filled hours of Friday standstill traffic, when the original plan had been to meet halfway between New York City and New Hampshire to avoid exactly that."

"So, nothin' to it," I joked, using one of our family's phrases that had evolved over time to refer to those moments when doing each other favors turned into something you needed distance from to tell as a story with any kind of humor.

"Reminds me of when you asked me to pick up a prescription for you on my way home once," I said.

"Remind me," he said, needing to be amused.

"I walked down five extra blocks to the pharmacy where the lady said, 'Oh, we don't have a prescription counter on 89th. That's our store on 84th, so I walked down five more blocks. Then I waited in a queue for a customer needing all three employees. Finally, it was my turn, and they said your prescription wasn't filled, did I want to wait or come back?

"'How long will it take?' I asked politely.

"'Not long,' she said.

"'I'll wait.'

"'Pills or liquid?'

"'Um, pills.'

"'Is he on a health plan?' He gets a discount if he is.'

"'I have to pay?'

"'Only if you want the prescription.'

"'Do you accept American Express?'

"'No.'

"'I'll have to come back.'

"'Next.'

"'Wait, I think I have enough. No, I don't. How late are you open?'

"'Ten,' she said, pointing to a sign.

"'I'll be back,' I said, stepping out of the line.

"'Next,' she said, and I left without the prescription I was just stopping by to pick up on my way home."

"Oops," said Iain, a grin in his voice.

Quaintly enough, as we siblings got bigger, our favors did, too, and "Would you mind picking up some milk if you're on your way over?" eventually became "Wanna help me move?" Of course, if you'd known it was moving a sofa, a chest of drawers, and two twin beds up three flights of stairs with no elevator, you probably would've said, "Sorry, sweetie, I'm on my way to... Hawaii." But we never said that. Instead we said, "What time do want me there?" and showed up, and that's probably why we sibs feel as close as we do.

It's why I now owe Bruce big-time for finding an exact replacement wedding ring for the one Frédéric just lost swimming in the ocean. Bruce secretly sent it all the way to Madrid in time for our first wedding anniversary.

Apparently, it only took about twenty-seven hours of his precious time, between standing in line at the jewelry store to make sure he had the right ring, trying to speak to an actual person over the phone in Spanish customs, and then standing in line, again, at the post office because apparently no insurance company will insure a simple gold band across the Atlantic.

Oh, and Bruce doesn't speak Spanish.

"So nothin' to it," I concluded brightly at the end of his story. "OK fine," I added, hearing only silence on his end. "I owe ya one."

"What you owe me," Bruce said, deadpan, "is a car. I like the new Porsche."

"Oh, I heard Iain's swapping cars again," I said mischievously.

But honestly, Bruce knows that things will come around again. One day, he'll be the one in need, and us siblings will circle the wagons. Usually when it's the least convenient. But that's the glue that keeps our clan together, the fact that you can count on family. No matter what.

Appreciate someone's effort and time.

39.

Tucked into Your Pocket

GRANNY CALLED ME...GIGGLING.

Said she'd been so tickled to see a pink envelope with roses on it among the white bills in her mailbox. Then when she saw it was from me, recognizing my handwriting, instead of opening it right away, she tucked the letter into her apron pocket to save it for later, knowing that half the fun is looking forward to something.

Then she said that suddenly, she had felt rather energetic. Which she hadn't for some time.

Said that she whizzed right through washing the breakfast dishes, and started sweeping. Once the kitchen was done, she kept right on sweeping, all the way down the hallway, across the living room, through the dining room, and right out the patio door. Swept the patio too. Said she was just a little whirlwind with a broom.

Said she only paused a few times to pat my letter in her pocket. Then Granny thought she must really be on a roll because she put in a load of laundry and then began dusting to beat the band. Before she knew it, the whole downstairs smelled lemony and was shiny and boy, was Granddaddy going to be surprised.

Then Granny said that she went outside and sat down by the roses in her garden, and slipped my letter from her pocket.

And she just held it for a long moment, delighting in anticipation.

Then she got an idea.

And tucked my letter *back* into her pocket.

She'd use it to tidy upstairs tomorrow!

That's when Granny called me...giggling.

Stay in touch with those you care about.

40.

Just in Case You're Starving

I SWEAR, MOM CAN BE SO FUNNY.

She just called and told me a story about her recent trip visiting friends of friends for the first time. She said she'd gotten away without breakfast—hard to believe—but assumed she'd have lunch with them, since she'd be arriving at noon, so she didn't bother to stop for a snack along the way. However, when she arrived, they didn't offer her lunch. In fact, they didn't offer her anything at all, so she thought they must have already had lunch, and probably thought she had too.

Well, for sure, if they'd been hosts she already knew, she would've said something or made little hungry sounds, but she had never met these people before, so she didn't say anything.

Eventually, they did offer her water, so while she was sipping, she said she was pretending she was chewing, and while they were giving her a tour of their home, she said she couldn't help imagining the things as edible: the sofa, a giant hot dog; the armchair, an enormous cupcake, etc.

Well, despite her tummy rumbling saying, "Um, excuse me, haven't we forgotten something?" Mom and the couple spent a lovely afternoon talking in the garden.

Finally, it was dinnertime and Mom said she was half famished, but for heaven's sake, both of them were on new diets, so they had three lettuce leaves each with a single drop of dressing and a cracker—which they split—and that was dinner.

Mom said she was so hungry going to bed she felt positively giddy and thought she might just sit down with the plastic knife and fork she always keeps in her purse and have her whole tube of toothpaste all to herself.

In the morning—this was great—the husband had already left for work having had his full breakfast, the wife didn't eat breakfast, but she asked Mom politely, "Would you like some tea?"

What Mom wanted to say was, "Yes, please, but instead of cream and sugar, may I have a loaf of bread and pound of butter?" Bless her heart, she declined to stay for lunch, really, she must be going, but so nice to have finally met you.

Then Mom drove straight to the nearest hamburger joint and ordered one of everything, laughing herself silly now that she had a cheeseburger in each hand, and three more in her purse. I was nearly on the floor from laughing by the time Mom got to the end of her story.

At the same time, it seemed so wild because most people complain they gain a few pounds every time they visit Mom and Dad because they feed everybody. Even people delivering packages.

In fact, I think most people visit because they know they'll leave for the airport with a homemade sandwich, grapes, a juice box, and freshly baked cookies. Mom and Dad would just never dream of sending someone out into the world without food, because maybe your flight is serving a meal, or maybe it's not. Or maybe your flight gets canceled, and you'll be living on a patch of terminal carpet for the next two days while they de-ice the city.

It's just something we do, they say.

So I'm going to remember to always offer a guest something to eat and drink no matter what time of day they arrive, or how long they're staying, because for some reason, I'm always hungry the moment I walk out the door.

And when someone is staying with us? I'll make sure they know that the kitchen is always open, so please, help yourself. Plus, I'll send them off with a little picnic when they go. It really is such a loving thing to do. Besides, it'll increase Frédéric's and my chances that when we're guests somewhere, we'll only have to brush our teeth with our toothpaste.

Not split it.

Be a gracious host.

LIFE SKILL

#6. Looking for the Big Picture

Builds Understanding

41.

Like the Big Dipper

TAKE CARE OF STARRY NIGHTS...ONE MAY CHANGE YOU forever...

I was driving home one evening and, after exiting the freeway, I began winding my way through the Minnesota countryside and soon came out of a forest and onto an open stretch of road running along a sleepy farm. It looked so lovely and quiet, and for some reason I'll never know, I slowed down and pulled into the empty dirt road next to a corn field. I turned off my engine and headlights. Then I rolled down my window and sat quietly resting my chin on my folded forearms to better listen to the night.

Slowly, my eyes began adjusting to the dark.

How especially beautiful everything was this night: the immense moonless starry sky...the rustling leaves in the summer breeze...the soft shushing of the corn...

Gradually, I became aware of peepers peeping, bullfrogs blowing, crickets creaking, a distant gaggle of geese honking... and a feeling of lucidity came over me that I didn't expect and could not explain. Turning my gaze upward, I began contemplating the Milky Way.

All those stars...

I began thinking about how much *stuff* is up there: black holes...red giants...white dwarfs...terms I knew without really understanding how they worked. Yet I, sitting "down here," silently acknowledged that both organic and inorganic matter were being held together by invisible forces.

How beyond BIG it all is, I mused. *How beyond small I am compared to a star. How insignificant—*

And that's when I was interrupted.

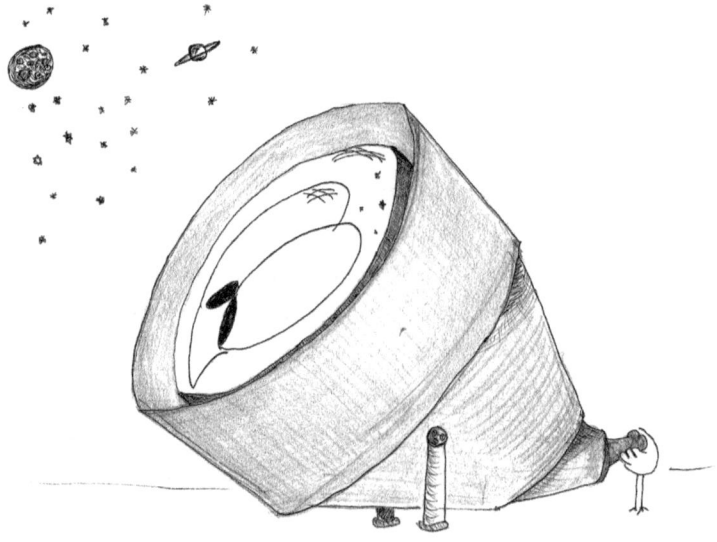

Even though the peepers were still peeping...

And the corn was still shushing...

From somewhere far away...the center of the Universe it seemed...yet at the same time...from within my own center...I sensed a message:

You're not insignificant.

You...are *conscious*.

Well, huh.

What a blessing lucid moments like this were, and I thought about the idea that stars are not mindful...and never would be...and teeny tiny though I might be...I could contemplate the Universe.

I knew I was looking...*up*.

Then I recognized the Big Dipper and for some reason, it looked more like a sieve than a ladle, this night.

"Oh," I said to the corn, "I want to be like that. Like the Big Dipper. I want to be a form capable of holding something important and let all the rest...flow right on through."

And with that, I turned on my car engine and headed for home.

Winding around the lakeshore, I couldn't stop thinking about my tiny revelation.

Compared to a star, I was smaller than small.

But I can *express* love.

Life can *do* something with that.

And although I know that stars will never be conscious in the way that I am, as I pulled into my driveway, I blew a kiss to the Big Dipper, and I could swear, it twinkled back at me.

Ponder why you're here.

42.

Broccoli for Breakfast

IT WAS GREEN. IT WAS HOT. IT WAS FRESH FROM THE garden. It had lemon butter on it, but no matter how we coaxed, Bruce, age four, he wouldn't eat his broccoli.

"Come on, Mr. Moose," Dad said encouragingly. "It's so much better when it's hot."

"Look, everyone's eating it," Mom added. "And you used to eat it when you were a baby, and now you're a big boy, and big boys try everything." Bruce shook his head. Dinner continued and we watched Walter Cronkite on the news until he said, "And that's the way it is," and we began clearing the table, getting ready for dessert.

All except Bruce and his broccoli.

It was hard seeing him staring at the now cold pieces on his plate while we were eating strawberry shortcake. But we kids all knew that if we didn't finish our plate for dinner, we could have it for breakfast, though that never actually happened.

Mom and Dad weren't being mean. They were just backing up against a principle. They knew that left to our own devices, we kids would be happy just eating cereal, pizza, and macaroni with cheese. As parents, they knew they had the responsibility of helping our bodies grow healthy and strong.

It was the reason they bought fresh produce when they could, made sure that we ate breakfast every morning, monitored that snacks were relatively healthy, planted a vegetable garden, and made sure we ate fresh fruit daily no matter the season, which also helped balance out the desserts we had—um, every night.

Still, ice cream wasn't a food group.

Once I remember not wanting to eat my salad, especially after little black football-shaped things appeared in them after Mom and Dad returned from photographing in Greece. I was moving them around on my plate, wondering how I could get them into my napkin without anyone seeing, when Mom said something like, "You know, every country has different foods and someday, you'll want to taste them, so it's a good habit to try new things now."

"Like olives," Dad said, taking Mom's cue, and spearing one with his fork. "Did you guys know that olives grow on trees?" Then he launched into the story of seeing their first olive trees in the distance, stopping their little rented car on the side of the road, Dad jumping over a stone wall, running across a small field, and sneaking a single black olive off the nearest tree branch. He excitedly popped it into his mouth, and then spit it right back out. Mom started laughing all over again.

"It was horrible," Dad said, making a funny face. "I had no idea the process it takes to make an olive ready to eat," he finished.

So, I speared one too.

"Hey, this isn't so bad," I said, which surprised the heck out of me.

OK, there are a few things I've tried now and will never try again, like raw oysters, which, after swallowing one, I learned are still alive. And octopus. Sorry, I just can't eat something *that* intelligent. And since Mom didn't prefer Brussels sprouts, I never had to eat them either, but if both parents liked something? Tough luck. You had to try it, so you didn't get into the habit of not trying new things.

Still, after the dishes were done and everyone except Bruce and his broccoli had left the kitchen, I snuck back in and ate it for him. I knew that I probably shouldn't have, but we kids had a little unspoken pact about helping each other out in moments like these.

But oh, wouldn't four-year-old Bruce have shaken his head in wonder to know that one day in his future, he'd not only be serving broccoli, perfectly prepared, to celebrate his first night cooking in his new apartment, but that he'd bring it proudly to the table for me, accompanied by his homemade hollandaise sauce.

Eat healthily.

43.

I'd Rather Vacuum than Floss

I KNOW, I SHOULD DO IT EVERY DAY.
I know, it's as important as brushing.
I know it comes mint-flavored and wax-covered, but until it comes chocolate-coated, I'm not interested.
I'd rather vacuum than floss.

I know that doing is a better way of teaching than telling and, in most cases, Mom and Dad understood that. We kids learned to eat healthily and be polite because Mom and Dad ate healthily and were polite with us. They modeled the behavior they wanted to help develop in us kids.
So, I can't figure out why I never learned to floss since Dad

flossed every night after dinner. Maybe it's because after you brush your teeth, your mouth's all clean, but then you floss, and your mouth's yucky again, so you have to brush again, and I just don't have that kind of time.

I tried flossing before I brushed once, but found half my dinner between my teeth, so maybe that's why I don't floss, albeit that's probably why one should.

In fact, I've only ever faithfully flossed several days in a row right before going to the dentist because by the third day, my gums hardly bled at all, so they didn't give me away that I didn't floss daily. But I never saw Mom floss, so I never felt guilty.

Then Douglas came along.

He flossed one day and got hooked on the stuff. He'd sit in front of his computer, a piece of floss hanging between his two front teeth, and occasionally he'd take his hands off the keyboard and saw it back and forth a bit. Lovely. The best was when he'd carry on a conversation with you and the floss was waving up and down.

Maybe that's why I don't floss.

Or it could be because I never understood the TV commercial where a white pearl necklace was stained blue from being baked in a blueberry pie. Then they came out all white again after being dropped into a glass with two fizzing tablets. I didn't understand how the tablets cleaned your teeth. What were you supposed to do? Put the tablets in your mouth, drink some water, and let your teeth fizz? I didn't get it.

So one day I asked Mom why she didn't floss, and she said sheepishly, "I know I should. I'm going to start tonight because all your grandparents still have their own teeth and I'm kind of attached to mine too." And suddenly, I understood the commercial.

So, I'm rethinking this flossing thing because flossing with

Dad the other evening, I found what amounted to a small salad in what I thought was my perfectly clean mouth after brushing.

Then it occurred to me that flossing was like gardening.

If you have a garden, you don't tend some of the plants and neglect the others. You want the whole garden to thrive, so I should start taking care of all my parts too.

Which means flossing tonight.

So the pattern eventually becomes automatic.

So I can model it for little ones one day.

Still, if you ever find any floss that's chocolate-coated, let me know.

Take good care of your teeth.

44.

Slouching

"SIT UP STRAIGHT, SWEETIE, YOU'RE SLOUCHING," SAID Dad good-naturedly, coming into the kitchen where I was about to make an after-school snack.

"No, I'm not," I said, slouching. "I'm sleeping. Sitting up."

"I'd call that slouching," he repeated with a grin, opening up the fridge.

"How can you tell?" I asked, amused. "Because my tummy's caved in? My back round like a bowl? My shoulders hunched over like a turtle?"

"That," said Dad, "hey, do you—"

"Know," I interrupted, "that how we carry ourselves says something about us? That how we hold ourselves may even demonstrate our level of consciousness?"

"Want—" Dad continued.

"To know the bigger picture?" I continued. "Which is having healthy posture your whole life long."

"Me—" Dad tried.

"Meaning that mindfulness gets built into your muscles, so poise becomes automatic when you stand or sit tall," I finished for him. "Dad, I know all this," I said wearily. "I'm just so tired after track practice I can hardly sit up, much less nice 'n' tall. I don't think I even have the energy to chew," I concluded, and to emphasize this, I slouched forward, putting my head down on my folded arms as if they were a pillow.

"To make you a snack?" Dad finished patiently. "You looked tired there…slouching."

"Yes, please," I said appreciatively. "I'll take a grilled cheese sandwich." And getting more comfortable, I turned my head. "Now thiff is thlouching," I added, into my arms.

"I know you know, sweetie," Dad said, patting my shoulder. "I see how you walk and sit and carry yourself. I see your poise…"

But I don't remember hearing anything else. I only remember waking a bit later and finding a grilled cheese sandwich on a plate under an upside-down bowl in front of me. A heart shape cut into the middle.

Maintain healthy posture.

45.

Don't Start

I WASN'T SURE, SO I DIDN'T SAY ANYTHING.

It wasn't my place.

No one appointed me judge.

And she knew the bigger picture anyway, so it wasn't a question of education or information.

It was a question of choice.

The freedom we each have to choose.

Still, I had my metaphor ready just in case, hoping humor might help her get off the fence.

Once and for all.

So, I just sat silently next to her, our eyes closed with faces upturned to the sunshine reflecting off the snow, hoping to get a little vitamin D in the middle of winter.

But I was ready in case she did ask, "Sweetie, do you mind if I smoke?"

"That depends," I'd say sneakily. "Do you empty your vacuum cleaner?"

"Of course," I imagined she'd say.

"Why?" I'd ask.

"Because if you don't," she'd continue, "it gets filled with tiny particles of gook and crud and no air can get through and it can't do its job properly, sucking in fresh air. If you don't clean its filters, air can't be exchanged and the whole machine could seize up and break down. Maybe even burn out the motor, and then it's too late to fix it."

"Exactly," I'd agree.

That's what a nurse had shown us visiting our school once when I was ten, putting a fake cigarette into a dummy's mouth, making it pretend to smoke, then opening up the chest to show us what its lungs looked like after smoking for one year, five years, and ten.

The antismoking campaign wasn't about quitting.

It was about not starting.

Apparently, the research showed that getting kids to quit smoking wasn't very effective, but educating kids not to start was.

Sitting in the sunshine, my friend finally asked, "Do you… want some chocolate?" squeezing my hand without opening her eyes. "I quit, by the way. Last summer. For good."

But I didn't say anything.

It wasn't my place.

No one appointed me judge.

We each have the freedom to choose.

But I did squeeze her hand back in acknowledgment.

No one said I couldn't be happy.

Don't start smoking.

46.

Thoughts on Fire

I HAD A THOUGHT RECENTLY, AND IT WAS SLIGHTLY appalling. I realized that after spending twelve years in school, four years in college, and two more years in graduate school, with all that formal education, I don't remember most of it.

I'm serious. It's scary.

If you gave me a blank piece of paper to write down the most important dates, names, and battles of American history, label the bones in the human body, explain cell replication in the correct order, or translate the abbreviations of the periodic table, the paper might not get filled. At least not on both sides.

There were honestly days during middle school, particularly in biology class, when I wondered if my mind actually had a tiny hole in it somewhere, which was why I was retaining only half of what teachers were trying to put in.

Other times, my friend Jenna and I would walk out of a three-hour exam shaking our heads, confessing that if we had to take the same exam the next morning, too, we'd probably fail it. The information stuffed into our heads seemed like it had a half-life that went down to zero before lunchtime. Ironically, it took us each over a decade to pay back all our student loans.

But here's what I do remember of my years in school, those moments when I came home with my thoughts *on fire*.

Getting a good education, Dad said, didn't depend on spending money, and he should know because he was a university professor for sixteen years and had graduated from public school. Getting a good education, he reminded me, depended upon one *being curious*. For example, a flower's not going to tell you why it blooms in the springtime. It's just going to do its thing. It was up to me to find out how and why, if I *cared* enough.

Of course arriving in the classroom with all your curiosity intact, sometimes you still got stuck with a teacher so unimaginative and painfully boring, you'd rather be weeding your neighbor's garden, laying bricks, or sitting at the dentist. But then, those teachers probably wished they were too.

But oh, the miracle of a great teacher.

I'll never forget the day we read our first play in English class when I was twelve, *The Monkey's Paw*. We'd been struggling for weeks learning the different parts of English grammar, only to understand why when we began reading Act I. One had to learn *how* to write, in order *to* write. And to write with conviction. And flair.

Our teacher began reading the spooky tale aloud in a mysterious voice he'd never used before while teaching, and soon the classroom disappeared and gave way to the woods. We were so mesmerized that no one noticed that he'd begun creeping from behind his desk, rolling still seated on silent wheels. Suddenly, eyes ablaze, he began rolling wildly, racing around the room while still in his chair, acting out a dramatic chase scene, and we girls collectively screamed in utter surprise and pure delight.

Another amazing teacher had me in awe with how she could change her voice so dramatically with every new character, sometimes reading passages with such exuberance that she foamed at the mouth.

Then there was my favorite homeroom teacher, who also taught English history. This guy was tall, bald, and buff, with a closely clipped military-looking mustache, and Jenna and I used to joke that he parachuted out of Special Ops airplanes at night during vacations. Only to learn later that he did. He was also our track coach for three years, training us as if we were state champions. Until we were.

He was the first teacher who deconstructed every sentence I ever wrote in my essays and term papers, trying to teach me how to write. In addition, he'd annoyingly ask me to back up my original thinking with research, believing that being able to synthesize information from different sources into a single coherent thought was a life skill. Bless him. Furthermore, under his tutelage, I never read a book more difficult than *Eleanor of Aquitaine*—at age fourteen, making all subsequent books comparatively easy when I went to college and beyond.

Then there was my math teacher from China. He taught at a roar, and he literally wore the exact same pants, jacket, and tie every day, unless he had five of the same kind. He also made us wear a cardboard dunce cap—that we'd made—when we missed an answer, or he'd have us stand upon our chairs.

I bravely asked him once why one would ever need to know the distributive process in the practical world. He told us he wasn't teaching us about mathematics; he was teaching us *how to think*. He said that by developing our skills of adding, subtracting, multiplying, and dividing, our brains were learning the principles of calculating, predicting, and deducing, which were crucial to solving problems we'd encounter in the world beyond his classroom. It may be why I don't remember many historic and scientific details from eighteen years' worth of formal education.

I'm too busy thinking.
I'm too busy problem-solving.
I'm too busy discovering.
But I do remember my great teachers *still*.

I remember them leaping, creeping, chasing, roaring, waving, foaming, sweating, correcting, listening, questioning, and repeating themselves in order to give me the mental tools necessary to face Life's challenges and creatively come up with solutions.

"Extra credit for flair and original thinking," Mr. Guy said.

Huh...looking back, I guess I do remember a lot.

I could probably, I don't know, fill a book.

Yay.

Be curious.

47.

Crunchy Air

I LOVE BREAKFAST.

If I could get away with it, I'd eat it three times a day.

I love toast, butter, jam, eggs, English muffins, pancakes, waffles, yogurt, orange juice, fresh fruit, cereal, and maple syrup over all of it, just as long as it's real.

But when I was growing up, I just didn't want it before leaving for school.

"The sun's not even awake," I'd whine when Dad would ask how I wanted my egg too early in the morning. But that was the rule. Breakfast was the most important meal of the day, and yer not walkin' out the door until that egg disappeared off yer plate. I thought about asking why we couldn't have Pop Tarts like kids ate on TV, or at least one of those cereals with a surprise in the box, but I already knew the answer. "Crunchy sugar-coated air isn't food," said Dad, handing me a piece of toast to mop up my fried egg. "You need brain food in the morning so you can think."

So, every day, he and Mom made sure we kids had breakfast, knowing we'd be happier if we did. The crazy thing is, whenever

I did manage to sneak out without it, later on the school bus I'd think, "Waa, now I'm hungry."

But sometimes I really did oversleep and racing around getting ready, I'd say, "Mom, I really don't have time for breakfast or I'm gonna miss the bus and then you'll have to drive me," which would have been pretty long in rush hour. So Mom and Dad began to get inventive.

Once Dad put a fried egg between two pieces of toast, wrapped it in a napkin, and handed it to me as a sandwich as I raced out the door.

The next time I was late, I got a breakfast sandwich in a little plastic baggie so the scrambled eggs didn't fall out, which I ate while running down the driveway. But when I found that grape jelly was now mixing with the chives in the eggs, I vowed to set my alarm back, concerned that the next time I was late, I'd get an egg, cheddar cheese, strawberry jam, and toast shake. With a straw. I managed to sit down to eat breakfast after that, usually with Dad.

But then came a morning when Mom saw me running around still stuffing schoolbooks into my backpack, so she simply met me at the front door with my full breakfast on a plate, handed me a fork and napkin, and had me drink some orange juice to wash down the breakfast I was about to eat.

"What do I do with the plaaate?" I yelled over my shoulder, eating as I ran down our eighth of a mile long driveway.

"Put it in the mailboooox," Mom called back, and I thought, *Won't Mr. Mailman be surprised!*

I don't remember when eggs got replaced by high-fiber cereals—I only remember there were still no surprises in the box. Then came Mom's yogurt craze, which soon, I shared too. I'd eat it for breakfast, after school, before bedtime, and standing up in front of the refrigerator with a spoon. Then whole wheat bread arrived on the horizon, and I never missed breakfast again.

But when Mom tried to replace butter with margarine, she almost had a mutiny on her hands.

"It doesn't even melt," said Dad, as we looked forlornly at our hot toast with an unmelted pat—which made us both suspicious. Nutrition is important, we argued with Mom, but if it doesn't taste good, we're not going to eat it, and with that, butter was voted back in.

Which is why Mom and Dad would be so happy knowing that even as a busy graduate student, I still wake up early enough every morning to eat breakfast so I have brain food. Sometimes, I even eat it three times a day, because it's all I can afford.

But that's fine with me. I flipping love breakfast.

Eat breakfast daily.

48.

Chocolate Melts

IT WAS SO DARK, I NEEDED A FLASHLIGHT TO LOOK for my flashlight.

Of course, it was ridiculous rummaging around in the back of my car even looking, knowing my emergency car kit wasn't there. Very helpful now that I'd run out of gas, at two in the morning, in the middle of a Minnesota winter, coming home from a club.

Dad was going to be thrilled.

I began my trek toward the nearest lights in the distance, hoping it was an open gas station, or at least a place to call home because I'd freeze staying in my car. As I walked in my boots, grateful I wasn't wearing heels that night, I thought, with some chagrin, about the specific things Mom and Dad had helped us kids put together to keep in our car when we began driving. You know, in case we ever broke down and were stranded.

1. *A flashlight.* Because think how much fun it would be to change a tire, and how much more fun it'd be to change one at night in the countryside with no streetlights nearby, which is when most tires like to go flat. Oh, and that little bulb

under your car hood? It gives you about as much light as a star does to read by. Also, having a flashlight is safer if you have to walk along the road. At night. Looking for a phone.
2. *Money.* A twenty won't get you far, but it's better than arriving somewhere empty-handed, and what you need is sold by someone who doesn't accept credit cards and there's no cash machine around.
3. *Water.* Because maybe you break down in the middle of nowhere and that weird thing happens when your throat suddenly goes dry and you feel like you're choking. You need liquid. Windshield wiper fluid won't work. Even a little water bottle will do the job. But only if you're a little bit thirsty. So better make it a bigger bottle.
4. *Food.* Something nonperishable like Spam. OK, not Spam, but maybe a can of peanuts or granola bars or fruit rolls. Something that lasts through different seasons. But don't take something too yummy, like chocolate bars, or else you'll keep pulling over to get one every time you go somewhere, and then they're gone, and you don't have any more for an emergency. Also, I found out that chocolate *melts.*
5. *A first aid kit.* It's important to have cream for burns, pain reliever for headaches, and adhesive bandages for cuts or a blister that you only get when you're in the middle of nowhere with no drugstore in sight. It's also good to know a bit about first aid, such as how to make a tourniquet out of your bra or shirt if you have to, and how to bandage a serious cut.
6. *An old towel.* There's nothing like having just changed a flat tire or rooted around in your engine trying to find out who's the wise guy not doing his job and why your engine just stopped, with nothing to wipe your hands on but your white shirt.
7. *A book.* If you've broken down and you have something to read other than your car manual, you're less likely to feel like

you're wasting your time waiting for a tow or sitting at a gas station. Because maybe they're going to repair your car right away, or it could still be an hour, or all afternoon because the part your car needs is not only made in Greenland, but also, it's still there. Imagine you're on a beach reading somewhere. It helps.

8. *Jumper cables.* Not essential, but holy cow, it's so much easier to find a jump if you find yourself with a dead battery and you already have the cables. But if no one stops right away, I recommend hanging them around your neck and twirling one end for attention.
9. *A blanket.* In the spring, summer, or fall, it can be used for a spontaneous picnic, but in the winter, it could save your life. Especially in Minnesota. Dad always said, "Dress like you'll have to walk a few miles, and have a wool blanket in the car in case you have to wait to be rescued." This wise advice made me change from my loafers showing bare ankles into heavy socks and hiking boots one winter morning before school. I also checked to make sure my car blanket was, in fact, still in the car, which for some reason it wasn't, so I was glad I checked, wondering how the heck it had gotten into the front hall closet on its own.
10. *A small duffle bag.* This item is the handiest of all because it keeps all the car emergency items neatly together, making it more likely you'll keep the kit in the car, where I've finally learned it works the best.

My theory is that if you have the stuff, you probably won't need it; if you don't have the stuff, you will.

Mom and Dad's theory is that if you have the stuff, you'll almost certainly use it, so take whatever you're going to need.

Additionally, they taught us that driving was invariably a time to practice looking for the bigger picture. Once behind the wheel, it wasn't enough just to be looking ahead. You had to be aware of all that was going on around you, including what might be coming up over the hill and around the bend. Driving was a time to anticipate situations, including the actions of others, and the more we practiced this, the safer drivers we became.

When Dad came to rescue me at the gas station—where the nice man allowed me to make a free call since the pay phone didn't accept credit cards, and I had no cash—I'll never, ever forget how dear Dad was. He even started laughing as he watched me try to figure out how to get the gasoline from the plastic gallon container he'd brought from home into my car tank.

I had suggested a straw.

Chuckling, he unscrewed the container's cap, turned it around, and voilà, it became a spout. Then it screwed back onto the container, making it a pitcher, allowing me to pour just enough gas into my car to make it to the station. Genius.

"Pa," I said, holding the flashlight from his car emergency kit in one hand and a funnel—also from his kit—with the other. "How come you're always so prepared for things?"

"Just comes with living a while, I guess." He sighed, amused. "A lesson's worth the most if you remember it. That's what turns it into wisdom."

So now, I'm all set if my car breaks down in the middle of nowhere, because I have everything I might need to be comfortable waiting for a tow or while my engine is being fixed, handily in my emergency car kit duffle bag.

Including my newest addition of a box of wet tissues.

Perfect for getting the melted chocolate off my hands.

Have an emergency car kit.

LIFE SKILL

#7. Watching Which Way We're Going

Builds Responsibility

49.

Being With

IT'S ONE OF MY EARLIEST MEMORIES...

Mom was taking wet laundry from the washing machine and putting a small pile on top of the dryer door, which opened out like a dishwasher's. I'd push the small pile forward into the dryer.

"Oh, *thank you*," said Mom, smiling down at me. "What a little helper you are." I was happy. I was helping. I was three or four.

"You were happy being appreciated," said Mom, smiling at the memory too. "Of course, it took patience to let your little hands stir the soup, put the letters in the mailbox, or push an elevator button after lifting you up," she admitted. Yet somehow she knew we children just wanted to be *with* her. Doing whatever she was doing.

Dad often painted a painting in his studio, with one of us kids set up next to him painting. I even remember that sometimes on a quiet Sunday morning, I'd find him in his studio doing a watercolor, and before I knew it, I was sitting on his lap, buttoned partly into his sweater so my arms were still free, with a fresh piece of paper where his used to be. Being little, it never occurred to me that he'd just stopped midstroke so we could do one together.

Around my fourth or fifth Christmas, I couldn't really assist Dad in his studio as he made silk-screen prints, but I still just wanted to be there. I was too small to clip the prints to dry onto the clothesline hanging behind his head, but I could clip the wooden clothespins onto the back of Dad's smock. Thinking I was being so sneaky and quiet, I never thought he knew what I was doing. Of course he did, and once I'd lined one side of his smock, he'd start chuckling and I'd start giggling, and it turned into our little game. All because he allowed me to stay.

Then last year, Dad visited me in Spain for the first time and while he was making a painting of the Pyrenees, I snuck up behind him on the grassy hillside and clipped one lone clothespin to the back of his shorts. Countless years had passed since our little game, but his laugh sounded just the same.

So when Mom had errands to do? Who did she find already belted into the car when she got there? *Moi.* (Me.) Dad had work to do outside in the carport? That's just where we kids wanted to be. Once I heard Mom start playing the piano, and I raced downstairs and scooted onto the bench beside her. She couldn't believe it. She played once in a decade, but the moment she'd actually managed to sit down, a little person had materialized next to her. I didn't want to play. I just wanted to be there. And I was willing to be absolutely invisible, if only I could stay.

When Bruce and Douglas came along, Christopher, Iain, and I did a lot of little-brother-sitting, and without even realizing what we were repeating, we included them whenever we could. Christopher took Bruce into the darkroom as he developed his black-and-white photographs. Iain rode Douglas around on his lap while cutting the grass. I'd pull around two chairs so they could see over the counter and help me make a dessert.

"How else would you have learned to do something that was real?" Mom asked when we talked about my memories. "You didn't want to crack a pretend plastic egg. You wanted to crack a real egg. You didn't want to play with an empty nail box. You wanted to hammer on the nail. Little people are so intelligent. You *knew* if something was meaningful or not." So each of my little brothers got an egg to crack into the bowl, and I'd scoop out the pieces of shell from the cake mix.

Once beginning to unload the dishwasher, Bruce, age two, appeared. Without a word, he retrieved a dinner plate almost as big as he was. I looked down at him. He grinned up at me, holding the plate tightly to his chest. Then he held it out to me. *Pling* went my heartstring. He just wanted to help. He wasn't asking me to hurry up so we could play. He thought we were playing. So plate by plate, cup by cup, we unloaded the dishwasher together accompanied by my "Oh, thank you" and "What a nice job you're doing."

Then I got the broom to sweep the kitchen floor, and he walked out of the kitchen without saying a word. A moment later, he was back with a broom just his size I didn't even know we had. I watched him wiggle the broom back and forth around the kitchen, walk through the pile I'd just made to go get that crumb over there, and bring it back with his broom, walking through my pile again.

But how else do we encourage hands to want to help? It starts at home. Too often we'd rather just get a job done. Do it quickly ourselves. But perhaps we lose the chance to reinforce the pattern of participation in little ones. Of *wanting* to help.

I handed Bruce the dustpan to hold while I swept up the piles. Then I opened the trash can so he could empty the dustpan. Which he did. Half into the trash and half back onto the floor. Oh, well, he was happy. He was helping. He was *being with*.

Allow others to participate.

50.

Not without That Chicken

"SAY WHATEVER YOU WANT," JENNA SAID, "BUT I'M NOT leavin' here without that chicken." And she folded her arms across her chest.

"Who eats other people's leftovers?" I hissed across the table in the café.

"Someone who just spent her food money on a little black dress," she pointed out.

"Well, you just spent yours on sunglasses," I countered.

"Exactly," said Jenna. "This is how we get back on track."

Twenty-five dollars a day. Each.

That's all we had to put a roof over our heads, eat three meals, and visit the local museum, palace, or ruin, depending on the city. It was 1988, and my friend and I were following *Let's Go Europe on $25 a Day* as if it was the Bible. We'd each worked several jobs after college, but neither of us had found our true purpose in Life, so we thought backpacking across Europe might help.

Ten months earlier, immediately after receiving a generous

invitation from my cousin twice removed who was stationed with the navy in Gaeta, Italy, offering his flat as a home base, Jenna and I were marking all the places we wanted to visit on a colorful map of Europe that covered most of the dining room table.

To save up for our big trip, I moved back home to work for Mom and Dad, and Jenna moved out of her cute flat in Chicago and in with a friend and onto her...floor. After nearly a year working full-time and saving every cent, not even willing to spend six dollars to go to the movies, the following spring, we'd both earned enough to fly across the ocean, purchase a three-month Eurail train pass, and pay three months of student and car loans in advance.

"Still," said Jenna, when we landed in Brussels on our first day at the end of March, "let's eat every other day so we can make it to Octoberfest, which I heard is in September."

"Deal," I said, having never skipped a meal in my life.

Mom helped us significantly in creating our budget, including suggesting an additional column titled "Unexpected," adding a full month of work to our proposed calendar, since it was an extra 10 percent of our original budget.

She'd counseled that things usually happened when you least expected them, often cost double, and when banks were closed. A little extra padding in our budget was being financially responsible, she maintained, literally able to respond to missing the last bus, finding the train full, becoming ill, or just being stuck somewhere, without everything else being thrown off-kilter.

Still, I never imagined stealing a half-eaten chicken from a recently vacated table in a cute Italian café, but of course, I did, which then Jenna arranged daintily between us. We were sure no one saw us, until a passing waiter silently placed a half-empty, but to us half-full, breadbasket on our table too.

"We really must get back on budget," said Jenna, waving her drumstick at me and slipping her new sunglasses up higher on her head so they wouldn't get greasy.

"We really must," I said, trying not to lick my fingers but failing, "because I also saw some sandals in the window next door."

Amazingly, we ended up traveling for two extra months beyond our plan, adding to our Unexpected column along the way by milking cows in Switzerland, babysitting in France, giving English lessons in Germany, sitting up on night trains across Spain, and once, I was even talked into singing for our supper in the Basque region of San Sebastián.

We even made it all the way to Octoberfest, which really is in September, and who knew that roast chicken was a traditional part of the German menu overflowing with Weissbeer, and gratefully, Jenna and I didn't leave without it.

Be responsible with money.

51.

Who's Wearing My Raincoat?

I WAS SURE IT WOULD BE THERE, BUT IT WASN'T.

It was just gone.

There was only grass.

No coat.

"So who's wearing my raincoat?" I implored the sky as raindrops began to fall. I couldn't believe I was walking back to the car empty-handed. Mom was going to be so mad. I braced myself as I climbed into the car. "Probably someone's just taken it and I'll get it back next track practice," I said, sounding hopeful.

"Or someone's just taken it, period, and you'll never see it again," said Mom, thoroughly miffed, as we pulled out of the parking lot. "How could you be so careless? We just bought you that raincoat."

Lip-quivering sniff.

"Well, I didn't forget it on purpose," I began.

"Well, you didn't remember it on purpose either," Mom countered. "You probably just took it off without thinking at all." Which made my heart constrict a little because she was absolutely right. I'd whipped off my jacket while running on the track with no thought other than *I'm hot.*

"What happened to 'Always look behind you'?" Mom asked. "Do you know how much we paid for that parka?" I did, actually, because we'd just recently bought a matching one for Jenna as a thank-you for inviting me on a spring break trip to Chicago and St. Louis with her parents. My parka was blue like her eyes. Hers was green like mine.

We trained every day of vacation for the upcoming track season, and watching us run one afternoon, her father said he thought we were fast enough to run up and over the St. Louis Arch. We were fifteen.

"And now we'll have to replace it, which is real money," Mom said, and the scenery spinning by snapped into focus. I hadn't thought about replacing it, and somewhere in my teenage consciousness, a window opened and a new awareness wafted in. We were seven in our family. Seven times anything added up. I'd never really thought about it before.

"Mom," I said, suddenly sitting up, "I'm so sorry for forgetting my parka, and I'll earn a new one working on the weekends. You taught me better. I should've been more careful." We kids all had long job lists to do on Saturday mornings, but washing windows, carrying firewood, and numbering photographic slides in the studio were things we got paid for.

"Deal," said Mom, finally looking over at me.

Well, who knew how long an hour really feels while washing windows or carrying firewood uphill, across a bridge, over a swamp, up another hill, and stacking it by the swing set? But I earned my new blue parka myself and wore it for more than a decade.

So wasn't I surprised to find it in Mom and Dad's front hall closet nearly twenty years later, when looking for something to wear to go for a walk one day with Mom.

"You still have this?" I asked incredulously, holding it up.

"It's not waterproof anymore, of course," said Mom, touching it with affection. "But I like wearing it sometimes as a windbreaker, knowing all the places it's been with *you* in it."

Heart-quivering sniff.

Take care of your things.

52.

Who Had Toast?

"OK, WHO HAD TOAST?" ASKED MOM, AND I CONSIDered stuffing the evidence in my back pocket, but there was raspberry jam on it. I peeked my head around the kitchen door.

"Uh," I said, meekly holding up my index finger, "that'd be me."

"Well, me," she said, narrowing her eyes but not truly mad, "in case you hadn't noticed, this kitchen was clean, and the polite thing to do is to leave things as clean as you find them, or cleaner." And with that, she deftly swiped the toast crumbs into the sink and walked out. Watching her go, I thought, *Mom, you're so cool. You hardly ever get upset about stuff like this. I wanna be like you when I grow up.*

The next day, I was unloading the dishwasher, and Mom, standing in the hall, looked down at the carpet and said, "OK, who's got muddy shoes? There are clumps of dirt everywhere." I looked down at my feet. Didn't look dirty to me. I lifted up my right shoe and looked at the sole. Mud. Yesterday's garden mud had dried in the treads of my hiking boots. I was leaving little tractor tire dirt patterns all over the house. Easy enough to pick up if you saw them before someone stepped on it. But then, who ever looked down at the floor? Mom.

Another time, Mom walked into the kitchen and found apple peelings in the sink, a jar of pickles on the counter, peanut butter, a pot of honey, a box of cereal, and two dirty bowls on the kitchen table, when she could've sworn the kitchen had been clean after lunch.

She came down the hallway knocking on all our doors, saying, "If you're someone who had a little snack but forgot to clean it up, it's still waiting for you," at which Iain, Bruce, Douglas, and I fell into single-file formation following her back to the kitchen.

While we were each cleaning up our own mess, Mom said reasonably, "Guys, this is just about being responsible, which includes cleaning up after yourselves. It's not only polite, it makes it nicer for everyone else, especially the person who cleaned things up in the first place." No big deal. No lecture. Just a lesson reinforced.

But it's funny, though, you never really understand certain things until you experience them for yourself. One Saturday afternoon, we seven had been working in the garden, and after lunch, the kitchen was a mess. But on this particular day, Mom and Dad said that cleaning it up could wait until after our naps, and sleepily trundled off to bed.

Everyone except me. I wasn't sleepy.

And partly because I knew it'd be a nice surprise for everyone, and partly because you never knew when brownie points would come in handy with Mom, I cleaned the kitchen myself. Well, everyone was happily surprised, but later that afternoon, in my perfectly clean kitchen, I found a jar of jam and some bread crumbs dotting my otherwise spotless kitchen counter.

"OK, who had toast?" I asked, finding the tiny mess downright unneighborly.

"Um, that'd be me," said Dad, peeking his head around the kitchen door.

"Well, me," I drawled, narrowing my eyes but not really mad, "whattsa big idea? In case you hadn't noticed, this kitchen was clean, and the polite thing to do is to leave things as clean as you found them, or cleaner." Dad nodded as I put the jam away and deftly swept the toast crumbs into the sink, probably thinking as he watched me, *You're so cool. You hardly ever get upset about stuff like this. I wanna be like you when I grow up.*

Tidy up after yourself.

53.

Butter on Your Elbow

SOMEWHERE IN THE UNIVERSE, A SWITCH MUST HAVE gotten thrown because the night before, we seven ate dinner at the table as we always did, but tonight, Mom corrected us every time we did something wrong. By the time I actually ate my first bite, my food was cold. It might have had something to do with the fact that I'd been talking with food in my mouth, Dad had burped, Douglas's plate looked a mess because he'd cut up all his food at once, Bruce had taken too big a bite so was chewing with chipmunk cheeks, Iain and Christopher had both their elbows on the table eating their corn on the cob, and I had just reached across Mom's plate to get the salt instead of politely asking for it to be passed, getting butter from her mashed potatoes on my elbow. Could be.

"And since when did you guys start leaning down to eat?" Mom asked, looking around incredulously. "We sit up straight at the table and bring our utensils *up* to our mouths." Five family members suddenly sat up a whole lot taller at the table. Maybe six.

Now, since Dad's default was eating too fast so he sometimes had a little something on his chin during a meal, he left table manners up to Mom.

"It's just what we do to be respectful," said Mom, ending her impromptu lecture on manners with a grin, gently wiping off a kernel of corn from Dad's cheek with her napkin that she'd forgotten to put in her lap.

Practice good manners.

54.

Thinking Drinking

"WANNA BEER?" A BOY ASKED POLITELY.

"No, thanks," I replied politely back, crossing the threshold into my first college dorm party. I was a bit nervous. I knew exactly no one.

"Fruit punch?" he asked brightly.

"Oh, sure," I said. "I didn't know there was punch." And I followed him into the...bathroom. He leaned over and dunked a plastic cup into the bathtub, which was filled to the top with a bright orange drink.

Wow, college.

"Enjoy the party," he said, handing me the dripping cup, and off he went. It tasted just like it looked: bright orange. Still, I felt less awkward holding a cup.

The music was already so loud you had to yell your name to the person who just asked you yours, but strangely, after a few more sips of my very orange drink, I wasn't feeling so shy anymore. I yelled to a guy asking if he wanted to dance, and he yelled back that he did.

Wow, I thought, feeling a funny sensation begin in my head.

This is fun! Why haven't I tried drinking sooner? Then someone handed me a second cup of punch, seeing my first cup was empty.

A few songs later, someone else came through the crowd with a tray of cups, and I neatly nicked one as he passed by because now it was getting hot in here, and I was actually thirsty.

That made three.

Then a friend appeared and asked if I was having fun, and I told her I was having a grrrrreat time and nearly knocked us both over slinging my arm around her neck giving her a hug.

But the very next moment, I wasn't feeling so great. In fact, now my head felt strangely disconnected from my body, and I was starting to feel nauseous.

"Excuse me," I said to no one in particular. "I'll be right back." I left the dorm room and began to ricochet down the hallway unable to walk a straight line, and two girls I didn't know heading for the party turned around and began to escort me.

"Wow, are those my feet down there because I can't really tell," I said, and then suddenly, I knew I was going to be sick and they raced me into the girl's bathroom.

In a bathroom stall on my knees vomiting, all I could think was, *Oh, yeah, this is great. Drinking's a blast. I can see why I should do this for fun*, while the girls patted my back tenderly and held my hair out of the toilet bowl.

Later, they helped me to bed, and after thanking them, I lay alone in the dark crying, missing the party, and feeling horribly sick in my room that would not stop spinning.

The next morning, my head felt like a bowling ball.

My eyes would hardly open.

Even my thoughts hurt.

But thinking about drinking I did.

I realized that it's a very personal journey, learning your safety limits when it comes to a substance created to *alter your natu-*

ral state. Despite cautionary tales from others, understanding my limits was something I needed to learn firsthand in order to internalize them. Thus commenced my somewhat turbulent journey of self-discovery regarding my relationship with alcohol.

It took me longer than I care to admit to recognize and respect the boundaries that I realize now are crucial for my safety. Boundaries unique to each individual. I acknowledge that what is my responsible alcohol limit is mine, and mine alone. Literally, it is that which still allows me to be *able to respond intelligently* should a situation or crisis arise. It's up to me to carry that wisdom forward. Gratefully, forward just happens to be the direction I'd most rather go.

Be responsible with alcohol.

55.

Mail Plane

"QUICK, PACK YOUR BAG," FRÉDÉRIC SAID. "A TINY ONE."
"Where am I going?" I said, not missing a beat. We often joked like this during our quick phone calls across the Atlantic since every minute cost dearly.

"To see me for the weekend," he answered. This made me smile. He was in Spain. I was in the States. The fact that we were separated by an ocean while I was in graduate school made the first two years of our married life more interesting.

"We can't afford it," I reminded him. "Especially for a weekend."

"I found you a super cheap flight," he countered, "on a mail plane."

I paused, not sure I'd heard him correctly. Then I smiled.

"But I'm female."

"I'm serious," he said seriously. "The flight leaves Friday morning, as in tomorrow at sunrise. You return Monday afternoon. Thirty-nine dollars. Round trip. OK?"

"For that price, I'm exactly where on the plane?" I asked. "In the hold? With the luggage?"

"Nope, you can't take luggage," he explained. "Just one bag that fits under your seat. The courier company will use your space in the hold for a package you'll deliver once you land."

"I have to deliver a package?" I asked suspiciously. "Sounds a bit sketchy, no? What's in the package?"

"No idea," he admitted. "But the company said everything's legal."

"They all say that," I said.

"And you have to take a package back with you," he added. It sounded dodgier all the time. Still, the proposal was tempting because we could only afford to see each other every four months during school breaks as it was.

Then the state of my room came into focus.

"Sweetie," I said, my heart sinking, "I just can't. Not this weekend. I just finished my last exam and my room is a wreck. I have no clean clothes. The kitchen should be roped off. Even I won't use my bathroom. I can't leave things like this. It also wouldn't be fair to my roommate." He was so disappointed, and I realized in that moment that when things are truly tidy and organized, there is a freedom to be spontaneous.

Had my apartment been all clean, Frédéric wouldn't have cared if I'd arrived in smelly clothes. If my things had been organized, I could have stuffed a weekend's worth of outfits into my backpack, picked up my passport, and sashayed out the door, dropping the trash off on my way out.

I was that kind of girl.

I could turn on a dime and loved that spontaneity about myself.

But I could also be a real piggy and let things go.

Mom would've been appalled.

I was appalled.

My mouse-sized bedroom was cute but small. I only saw a six-inch square of sky if I was lying down on my bed. I didn't have the freedom to be messy. If one item was out of place, it literally took up my breathing space.

Happily, I'm quick on the draw and the following Friday, I was fastening my seat belt on the tiny mail plane, wondering if the big brown burlap bag in the net above my head was what I'd be delivering or held the parachute they'd teach me how to use after takeoff. Still, I was excited.

Ten hours later, I walked through security starving, having missed the memo that there was no food served on board, wondering in hindsight if the bag overhead had actually been full of peanuts and I was just supposed to have helped myself.

"How easy was that?" asked Frédéric, opening his arms.

"So easy," I lied, still not feeling my backside from the small plane's vibration. "We should do this every weekend."

"We should," he agreed seriously. "Where's the package?"

"You're holding it," I muffled into his chest, not having to deliver anything in the end. "I only have to be back Monday morning on time, or you'll have to mail me home in an envelope."

Who knew what freedom lay hidden in being truly organized, and what magic can accompany turning on a dime? Like going to Madrid for a weekend as mail.

Stay organized.

56.

Where's the Moose?

DAD WAS SPEEDING.

"One, two, three, four, five, six—" Mom counted aloud as the prairie grass began to blur outside the van windows again. "Wait!" she gasped, "Where's seven?" and we six all looked at each other. "Where's Bruce the Moose?" Mom squeaked, her voice rising an octave.

That's when Dad started speeding.

Mom and Dad were big on teaching us kids important lessons, especially ones having to do with outside the safety of home, so you didn't have to learn them the hard way. One was "Always look behind you" when leaving a place, so you didn't have to go back and retrieve what you'd forgotten.

Which is how Mom had gotten into the habit of counting heads each time we stopped and got out of the van to get gas, winkie, photograph, or just stretch our legs during our camping trip from Ohio to Wyoming during one summer vacation.

Dad raced to the next exit, but holy cow, there was no crossover, so he raced to the next exit, which felt like an eternity. We kids were absolutely silent in the car and Mom looked like she was holding her breath.

At the following exit, Dad tore across the highway pass, down the ramp, and back onto the freeway, passing the gas station we'd just left, but now on the other side of the freeway, so all we could do was zoom past. Fortunately, Mom and Dad were fast enough to see Bruce in the arms of a great bearded truck driver assuring us with his friendly wave that all was OK.

For the truck driver, not Bruce.

Bruce looked like he'd been…left.

So now I'm really good at looking behind me when I've been somewhere and which is why I still have my sweater from the restaurant, my umbrella from the café, my sunglasses from the taxi cab, my book from the park bench, and my reading glasses from the bookstore. And if I ever needed reinforcement for this handy little pattern, it came the other day after my plane landed.

I got the strangest feeling after looking behind me, to get down on the floor to look there, too, and it's why I still have my passport that must have hopped out of my purse while I was sleeping to have a seat with no window view all by itself.

"Where's the Moose?" Dad said, holding out his arms with a grin.

"I'm here!" Bruce said, his eyes shining with emotion. Mom and Dad hugged him tightly and then hugged the truck driver a huge thank-you too.

"One, two, three, four, five, six, and a Moose!" Mom sang out, and off we zoomed once again, to find mountains with snow in summertime.

Always look behind you.

LIFE SKILL

#8. Listening Within

Builds Wisdom

57.

Cucumbers in Her Purse

"MOM, DID YOU JUST PUT A CUCUMBER IN YOUR PURSE?" I asked, coming into the kitchen.

"No, I just put three cucumbers in my purse," she said, biting into a fourth one she'd just finished peeling. This strange new behavior of eating a cucumber like a banana had been going on for about two weeks now.

"What's going on with you?" I asked, truly concerned.

"No idea. My mouth just burns all the time now. This helps," she said, crunching and shaking her head.

"But that's so weird," I said. "You should see a doctor." She blinked and I could tell by the blank look on her face that the thought hadn't occurred to her yet. What amazed me more is that if one of us kids showed signs of being sick, she never hesitated to take us to the doctor. Moms: they do everything for everyone else, but rarely for themselves.

Also, Mom really cared about being healthy.

She never took up jogging or anything, but she and Dad made sure we kids went to bed at the same time every night when we were small, got eight hours of sleep, encouraged naps on the weekend, bundled us up in the cold, put hats on us under the summer sun, and annoyingly reminded us to drink water daily.

Additionally, she took us kids for annual medical check-ups to make sure we were growing properly, and to have a marker of good health for our backs, eyes, and ears, in case something ever changed, as it did with me when I started to have back pain as a teenager. An X-ray later showed I had slight scoliosis, and needed supports in my shoes during the years I was growing.

My first memory of going to the doctor's was when I was three or four. Mom told me that I was going to get a shot in my arm that would feel like a mosquito bite. But she also claimed that I was a big girl who knew how to hold the peace and that I was not to cry. Having been prepared, I didn't cry, and afterward in the car, Mom surprised me with a bag of four tiny chocolate-covered malt balls.

Yet no matter how vigilant Mom and Dad were to our health and safety, medical emergencies still occurred, and thank goodness, they knew when to call the doctor.

Once when Iain was fifteen, he began vomiting, and thinking he only had a stomach flu, Mom simply put him to bed, monitored him hourly, and made sure he was drinking fluids so he wouldn't get dehydrated. But twenty-four hours later, he was no better and now had a fever, so she called the doctor knowing you don't mess around with fevers.

Two hours later, Iain underwent emergency surgery for an infected appendix, normally the size of one's little finger. Iain's was the size of a small banana and about to burst. Mom was so upset that she hadn't known those two symptoms together, vomiting and fever, could mean appendicitis. She made a mental note of it and explained it carefully to the whole family that night. Good thing because only four months later, Bruce, six, displayed the same symptoms, and Mom recognized it in an hour, instead of a day.

But now it was my turn to be the mom.

"Let's make you a doctor's appointment right now," I suggested.

"OK," she crunched.

As it turned out, an ordinary blood test showed that Mom was insanely anemic and getting her on some daily iron pills removed the burning sensation in her mouth in no time.

"Mom," I said, as we drove home from the doctor's together, "how long has it been since you've had a full head-to-toe check-up?"

"I can't remember," she admitted sheepishly.

"Which tells us something," I said tenderly. "Promise me that we make an appointment as soon as we get home and that you begin to have them annually. You're too important to not be as healthy as possible." She promised she would. "Now, do you want a little surprise for being such a good girl at the doctor's?" I asked.

"Only if it's chocolate-covered and not a cucumber," she said with all sincerity, which was perfect, as I handed her a tiny bag of four chocolate-covered cashews. Her favorite.

Pay attention to your health.

58.

Una Siesta

"SOMEONE NEEDS A NAP," MOM SAID, STEERING TINY four- or five-year-old me up the stairs. I complained the whole way. Told her I didn't want a nap. I wasn't sleepy. Just kept whining and whining, the signal most parents know that means little people need a nap. She tucked grumpy me into bed, kissed my scowling forehead, and without further ado, closed the door, a tacit understanding that I was to stay put.

But not feeling tired and to exercise a little independence, I got back out of bed, took a box of tissues and began pulling them out, one by one, folding them into little cakes instead. After I'd emptied the box, feeling strangely sleepy, I crawled under my covers. It was dark when Mom woke me hours later for dinner.

Moms. Bless 'em.

This memory makes me smile now because snuggling down to take a nap was one of my favorite things to do as a teenager, and still is as an adult. In fact, some of my happiest memories are me tucked up cozily back to back with Mom on a lazy Sunday afternoon, especially hearing a summer storm coming.

Amusingly enough, discussing naps one day with her, I had no idea how important they were during her and Dad's beginning romance at college.

Mom lived comfortably at home with her parents while starting university, but eighteen-year-old Dad was completely on his own, working two jobs to pay for room, board, books, and classes as a full-time student.

Mom told me the story of Dad choosing morning classes, then riding the city bus across town to his drafting job, eating a quick lunch, working again until late afternoon, then riding the last bus back to campus, which if he missed it, meant an hour walk back home.

Then he'd study at the library, eat dinner, and go back to the library to get ahead, since he worked a second job on Saturdays. He only saw Mom on Sundays, sharing her family's noonday meal unless they studied together.

By sophomore year, Dad was so skinny and worn out, he bought an old car, enabling him to toodle back and forth between campus and work. But the best part of the car was that it not only had window shades that pulled down, but the driver's seat reclined all the way back, so Dad could sneak out to his car at lunchtime, wolf down a sandwich, then take a power nap for ten to twenty minutes, which saved him. For Dad, naps worked wonders. It was a tradition he began at college, and Dad's sure he's never missed a nap since, saying that without one after lunch, living almost hurts.

Over the years listening to my body, I've found that even just pausing and closing my eyes, relaxing my muscles, and deepening my breathing for a few thoughtful minutes can quiet busy thoughts and reset my brain. With practice, I've taught myself that I don't always need to be horizontal and fall asleep to feel refreshed. Just closing my eyes to disconnect from my visual surroundings for a small while can be enough to make a difference for the rest of my day.

On the other hand, now living in Spain where the heat often reaches one hundred degrees in the middle of the day during summer, I've grown rather fond of one of their most cherished national traditions after lunch and never complain if I'm offered one: una siesta. Spanish for a nap. Bless 'em.

Naps can work wonders.

59.

Ah-Choo!

"AH-CHOO," I SNEEZED.

Mom and Dad exchanged looks and left the kitchen table where we'd been eating lunch together. I sat, bewildered. A moment later, they came back, each carrying something.

"How long have you been sick?" asked Mom, handing me a bottle of vitamin C.

"I don't know," I said. "A few days. But I don't seem to be getting any better."

"Well, I'm not a doctor," Mom began, "but if you have a cold, I wholly recommend taking vitamin C every four hours with plenty of water." She handed me a pitcher big enough to water a palm tree. "Vitamin C's water soluble, so whatever your body doesn't need, you'll winkie away." I looked at the bottle suspiciously, but then remembered how seldom Mom was sick.

"And here," said Dad, handing me a royal-blue heating pad across the table, "try pinning this inside your shirt to keep your chest cozy. "Keeping extra warm helps you heal, I swear," which he could do. The story went that when Dad was a baby during a cold Canadian winter, he'd become ill with pneumonia. The doctor making house calls that night said to my grandmother, "Forget about this one. He's not going to make it," but Grandmother had thought, *The hell he's not*, and had covered Dad's chest with a homemade mustard plaster, turning his skin bright red but saving his life. The next morning, the doctor said it was a miracle. Grandmother Dix said it was mustard.

I tucked the electric heating pad under my shirt and let Dad plug me in. A few moments later, I had to admit, it felt rather friendly.

"Oh, and I'm running you a hot bath," said Mom.

"Mom, it's only a cold," I said.

"No matter," said Dad. "A bath will raise your body temperature high enough to keep killing the germs that are making you sick. Get down in the water until you're up to your neck and stay there until you really sweat. Got a good book?"

"I do," I said, because I did.

"I could read to you," said Mom, which made me smile because that's what she used to do when I was a teenager with menstrual cramps.

"Mom, that's so sweet," I began, "but—"and then I yawned.

"And I'd recommend a nap today too," said Dad with a smile.

"I was just going to say that," said Mom. "Getting extra rest is probably the most important thing you can do to help the healing process."

"Listen to your body. That's what feelings are for," Dad added. "They're signals. They're trying to tell you something." Mom nodded in agreement, knowing that although her little girl was sick, at least she was home for the weekend.

So right after lunch, I had a hot bath while Mom read to me until I turned pink, drank enough
water until I sloshed, took some Vitamin C, and let Mom tuck me into bed for an afternoon nap. Dad had even put the heating pad under my sheets and plugged it in, so my bed was warm when I got in.

Back at school and for the next few days, I kept up the Vitamin C, dressed extra warmly, and managed to either take a nap or go to bed early. On the morning of the fourth day, my cold was gone, and I couldn't help blessing the wondrous process of healing. I also bought myself a heating pad with flowers on it for the next time I go, "Ah-choo."

Take extra care when you're sick.

60.

Black Ice

DON'T GO. STAY.

I heard the message as clear as a bell, but it was too late; I'd already offered them a ride. Still, it felt strange not paying attention to my center because I'm usually grateful for inner guidance.

"Sure, I can take you all the way to the city," I heard myself say to the two French boys trying to catch an early morning flight back to Paris for Christmas.

Don't make that promise.

But I'd already planned to drive down from Vermont to Connecticut to drop off my friend. For guys I hardly knew, I'd give up spending the night with her and continue on to New York City. It seemed like a thoughtful thing to do.

I couldn't have been more wrong.

Don't drive into the city.

There it was again. That warning.

But I didn't have time to listen. The snow was beginning to fall and we were already late getting on the road. Then it started to really snow. And snow. And Snow. And SNOW.

What was usually a four-hour ride zipping through four states in daylight turned into a plodding eight-hour slog in almost blinding slippery conditions. I was both physically and mentally exhausted, arriving late for dinner instead of an early lunch.

Don't go. Stay.

This was starting to be alarming.

I have to go, I told my inner self. *I made a promise.*

You shouldn't have.

They'll miss their flights, I insisted.

Not your responsibility. Safety is.

But what was I going to say? "Hey guys, I'm getting an inner message we should stay here tonight. Just a feeling. Sorry, you'll miss your flight home for the holidays."

That works.

But I didn't feel I could change course having made a promise. Also, no one had heard during dinner how the silent falling snow had turned into a strange tinkling sound, because by the time we were saying our goodbyes, both the strange sound and the snow had stopped altogether.

All was silent.

So, I didn't say a thing.

Hugging my friend goodbye, I yawned and one of the boys offered to drive the last hour into the city, which seemed like a good idea. But as I climbed into the back seat to let the other boy be the copilot, I heard the warning again.

Don't. Go. Stay.

The messages were louder, so I thought maybe the boys heard it too. That would get me off the hook.

Why me? I asked silently.

Because you're listening. They're not.

But the boys hadn't heard a thing, so I buckled up, closed my eyes, and hardly out of the driveway, I was asleep.

Suddenly, I was violently rocked awake as the car began

swerving, fishtailing this way and that, spinning out of control. I opened my eyes to see an enormous sycamore tree heading straight for us in full swirling force as my driver held down the brakes to no avail.

Black ice.

I braced for the impact, even though I was wearing my seatbelt, but suddenly, we lurched just as violently to a halt.

A few feet from the towering tree.

Somehow one lone tire had found a patch of gravel just big enough to grab the tire's tread before we went over the road's edge and onto the icy snow-covered grass and into the solid tree.

With my next heartbeat, I knew that this winter's night was not my time to graduate from the world.

Thankyouthankyouthankyou, I thought, shaking uncontrollably but now acutely awake. *You have my full attention now*, I said within, directly to Life. *Which way do you want me to go?*

My answer came in the form of a salt truck, telling us to follow him to the freeway, where he assured us that the roads were only wet. Only here on the empty country roads were there patches of ice, he pointed out.

It wasn't until the next day's news that I learned how many accidents there'd been in a tiny window of time in a remote town of Connecticut, one of them fatal.

"Well, sweetie," said Mom, looking over at me safe and sound in the kitchen, "looks like you left just in time."

You almost left forever.

I excused myself and went alone into the living room.

I'm listening, I said to Life, listening.

Feelings are signals and signals are to keep you safe. But if you're not willing to listen, what's their wisdom worth?

That got my attention.

So, I'm working at listening. Within.

Still.

※

Pay attention to inner messages.

61.

So Not OK

BLESS HER HEART, I COULD SEE THAT MOM WAS NOT OK.

I sat down on her bed and picked up her hand, squeezing it to let her know I was there for her. She tried to smile back, but she couldn't fool me. Mom was not fine and hadn't been for some time. Ever since Christopher had left for college, Mom had snooked the free room, a perfect set up it turned out, since Dad snored like a bear and liked to go to bed early, and Mom liked to stay up in the evening to read in bed.

When I think of the mother who raised me, my mental constellation is of a vivacious soul, busy as a beaver, her long, black hair parted in the middle and held back by a hair clip, her blue eyes sparkling behind her glasses.

What mattered to Mom most were matters of the heart.

In developing those things that are invisible to the eye. Our centers. And hers.

In fact, I hardly ever remember Mom looking at herself in the mirror. She was too busy mothering. She only wore makeup on Christmas or red lipstick if she had a dinner party. She didn't wear jewelry, except her wedding band, and pretty much lived in pants, T-shirts, and tennis shoes.

It's probably why she could move so fast.

Besides Dad, Mom never had any outside help raising us kids or cleaning the house, and when we were old enough, we became the help, doing our part to keep the household running and the garden growing, which didn't weed and water itself.

On top of everything else Mom did, she also became Dad's business partner, partly through osmosis and partly because Dad didn't know anything about bookkeeping and accounting and Mom did. So, when Wonder Woman appeared on TV when I was thirteen, I didn't think it was a coincidence that she looked a lot like Mom. Mom just wore tennis shoes, and I thought Wonder Woman could've run faster if she did too. Little did we know, things would change for Mom.

The summer I was eighteen, Mom began to feel unusually lethargic, and a blood test showed she was extremely anemic and had precancerous uterine cells. Her doctor performed a full hysterectomy in response without any replacement hormone treatment afterward, and Mom spiraled into a depression for the next, what she believes in hindsight, was twenty years.

Indeed, Bruce and Douglas feel that they were raised by a very different mother than us first three kids. Looking back now with less hormonal eyes, Mom said it still breaks her heart that, not knowing anything about depression, she didn't get a proper diagnosis or the emotional, physical, or medicinal help that she needed. She had gone to bookstores in desperation, but back then, shelves weren't filled with self-help books on the subject, so Mom simply suffered instead of getting support.

During those years of depression, she only knew that something was seriously wrong. Her every thought felt inexplicably and drastically altered, the light seemed dimmed, and joy felt drained away.

It's hard to be your own advocate when you're feeling unwell. If you don't have the energy or will to get out of bed, much less dress yourself, it's not any easier to find information about what might help you, and the internet didn't exist yet.

Day by day, Mom's world felt darker.

Nothing felt easy. Nothing felt fun.

And perhaps the scariest for her was the feeling that hope was fading away too. She didn't look forward to anything anymore, except us kids coming home for a visit.

Years later, what broke my own heart was hearing Mom describe how much she pretended she was OK, when she really wasn't.

On top of feeling miserable, she felt guilty too.

She was conscious what a privilege it was to have a loving, healthy husband, thriving kids, a safe, sturdy house, and interesting projects to work on in a new city with parks and lakes to discover. But with all this, she only felt oogie.

When I chose my exchange year from Middlebury to study psychology at the University of Minnesota, living at home for my junior year, I began to notice these changes in Mom.

After some very serious talks together and a few family meetings, finally Mom began seeing a therapist and receiving hormone replacement therapy. Additionally, she began getting outside for daily walks, which helped because Dad's absolute misreading of her lethargic condition and saying once, "If you feel depressed, why can't you just cheer up?" really didn't.

However, his giving her daily shoulder massages did help.

Little by little, things began to get back on track and though it took quite a few years, Mom became her smiling, beaverly self, typing away on her blue typewriter once again.

Still, we all asked her to make a promise, first to herself and then to us, that when we asked her, "Are you OK?" she would tell us the truth and would monitor herself as the years went by.

We reminded her that it's OK not to be OK, but it's not OK not to tell us, because being honest with how you feel may be the first step to getting back on the road to OK once again.

Be honest about your mental well-being.

62.

The Best in Me

"WENDY, WHY ARE YOU MARRYING FRÉDÉRIC?" ASKED Bruce out of the blue, sitting at the kitchen table one summer morning in August.

It was the day before my wedding, and I looked up from the sink where I was washing strawberries. His face looked so innocent and thoughtful, with no hint of challenge in his voice, that somehow just saying, "Because I love him," didn't seem adequate for the moment.

So, for one of the few times in my life, I actually managed to pause before speaking, and in pausing, turned quietly within.

"Because he brings out the best in me," I heard myself answer. "I love who I am with him. I am my highest self."

"Wow, good answer," said Bruce, grinning, his blue eyes shining, matching the lake beyond.

"Yeah, it was, wasn't it?" I said, turning back to the strawberries.

Over the four years I'd known Frédéric, I'd learned that I had chosen him not only because we loved one another, but because we inspired each other to be the best version of ourselves. Perhaps that's what being a soulmate is all about. Thanks, Mr. Moose, for asking.

Choose a partner who inspires your highest self.

63.

Ol' Coot

"ONE ONE THOUSAND, TWO ONE THOUSAND, THREE one thousand, four," I counted aloud. I was standing not quite waist deep in a Minnesota lake, about fifteen feet from shore, waiting for Dad to resurface.

"OK, so I'm going to roll over," Dad had explained earlier while slipping into his kayak. "And then you'll see me pat each side of my kayak to let you know I'm peaceful and not panicking. Then using my trusty paddle, I'll try to right myself back up. That's the plan."

"That's what your instructor taught you?" I asked, raising an eyebrow. "To pat your kayak while upside down underwater?"

"Yup." He nodded, buttoning down his spray skirt. "That way if you tip over, your paddling buddies know you're OK and you'll try to right yourself. If they don't see you pat your kayak, that's a signal you're not OK, and you need a rescue."

Exactly why I have never felt the desire to kayak, I thought.

Dad had learned how to roll over in a swimming pool the week before. Today he was trying it in the lake, hence my presence.

"So how long do I let you stay upside down if you can't roll yourself back up?" I asked.

"Oh, I can hold my breath for a good minute or so," he said, strapping on his helmet. I knew I'd start a rescue after fifteen seconds. Then with a grin and a wave of his paddle, Dad dumped over.

"Five one thousand, six one thousand, seven one thousand, eight," I continued.

Suddenly, Dad's hand appeared out of the water, and he slapped the kayak with a great *fwap-fwap!*

Then he slapped the other side. *Fwap-fwap!*

Then all was quiet again.

"Nine one thousand," I continued, watching carefully.

Then Dad broke through the surface paddling like crazy. He made it halfway up, gulped some air, then slid back down underwater again.

"Now what am I supposed to do?" I yelled to the underside of his kayak, "Start counting from one again?"

Dad appeared and disappeared a few more times, gulping air each time, flailing his paddle like an underwater gladiator fighting something fierce.

In spite of myself, I found myself admiring the scene, marveling not a little at Dad's lifestyle choices that had led him to this moment. He had always loved the great outdoors and had encouraged us kids to enjoy being outside and active, too, beginning by inviting us to be by his side when we were very small.

Dad taught us all how to ride bikes, swim, ice skate on a frozen lake, row a boat, paddle a canoe, and even downhill ski—which we older kids did exactly twice growing up because it was just too expensive. Without saying the actual words, Dad often convinced us to get off our butts and get outside, knowing that we'd feel much better running around playing kickball than watching stupid TV.

Later, listening to our bodies, we got off our own butts and preferred being outside. And when I began running in middle school to be on the track team? Who took up running too? Dad, at forty-seven, partly to keep me company, and partly to prove that he could still keep up. Which he could.

Having counted to fifteen seconds three different times, I was just about to help Dad flip over, when he rolled up all by himself.

"Woohoo!" I cheered.

"Nothin' to it," he sputtered. "Pretty good for an ol' coot, huh?" he asked, obviously proud.

"You are anything but an ol' coot, Pa," I said, meaning it. Dad had just turned sixty, and here he was, learning a new trick to have fun staying healthy. "In fact, you're a tough act to follow, but I intend to try," I added, beaming with admiration.

"In a kayak?" Dad asked hopefully.

"Uh, no," I said. "But we can go for a canoe ride when you're done dumping over. Go see if the beavers are back."

"Deal," he said, flopping over with a great splash.

One one thousand, two one thousand, three one thousand, four.

Exercise for fun and health.

64.

All Dressed Up and Nowhere to Sneeze

OH, GREAT. JUST GREAT.

The flight hadn't even taken off yet, and I could already smell cigarette smoke from the back of the plane. The idea of smoking and nonsmoking sections in a closed capsule that circulated air was probably the dumbest thing I knew. Seeing me shake my head while talking to myself, the guy who'd been sitting next to me got up and moved away one seat. Oh, well, he'd already been using my armrest without asking. I casually leaned over and smelled my armpits anyway.

"Someday," I sighed, trying to get comfy, "even transatlantic flights will be nonsmoking." Smoking had just been banned on national flights. How crazy to allow lighters to make tiny blazes on airplanes.

Oh, no, I realized with chagrin, *my book.* I had tucked it into the outside pocket of my suitcase just before jumping into the taxi and had forgotten to get it out before checking it. I began thumbing through the airline magazine to take my mind off getting lung cancer before landing.

Then I was cold.

"So smart," I continued aloud, "stuffing your sweater into your suitcase just before closing it only because you were hot packing." Maybe the article on Tahiti would help. By the third paragraph I was freezing but didn't want to ask for an airline blanket that other people had probably sneezed on because they were cold. They weren't exactly in vacuum-packed bags in the overhead. At least, not in my class.

"Why is it always freezing on airplanes?" I continued mumbling. "What's in the hold? Ice cream?" The guy who'd moved over one seat looked at me again, obviously alarmed I was still talking to myself. I laid my head back against the headrest, closed my eyes, and wished I was meeting Frédéric in Tahiti.

Then my neck hurt.

I turned my head to the left. Turned it back to the right. I scooted up a few inches to see if the headrest would fit my neck any better. Nope. I wondered why they didn't just attach a giant elastic band you could loop your head through and wear like a headband, keeping your head from falling forward if you did manage to fall asleep. I looked for a suggestion card.

Then I was thirsty.

"Perfect," I said to the empty seat next to me. "My water bottle. How could I have forgotten my water? I never go anywhere without water." I checked to see if it had gotten in my backpack by default. It hadn't. I turned around and looked down the aisle to see when the drink cart would reach me. Passengers were still playing stuff-the-bin above their neighbor. It'd be a while. I licked my lips and tried not to think about how much water they had in Tahiti.

Chapped lips.

Of course, my Chapstick was in my travel kit in my suitcase down with the ice cream, so I didn't even bother looking. I stretched my legs out the as best I could in the ten inches of space between me and the bulkhead. At least no one was going to recline their seat into my breathing space. It didn't matter I was so close to the wall that I couldn't see the whole screen at once. Then I yawned.

Bad breath.

So that's why the guy had moved over a seat. I had breathed on him. I should have bought those mints in the airport, but at three times the normal price, it was highway robbery. Still, it was a good thing I wasn't on the plane to find a date.

A couple across the aisle began eating what looked like homemade sandwiches. I thought about the things in my backpack and wondered if there was anything remotely edible in there. Probably not. My cherry Chapstick was in the hold. I had missed lunch, but it was better than missing the plane, and I comforted myself that they'd be serving dinner at some point. Oh joy, airplane food.

After three minutes, I was bored.

I opened my eyes and began counting the nuts and bolts on the wall in front of me.

Then my feet hurt.

I'd been wearing my boots all day.

"Another thing you handily forgot," I said aloud to the wall. "Your bunchy socks." I usually took a pair of thick socks to wear on a plane so my feet were warm and comfy, and I could pad around the place in style. I thought I'd been very clever to start bringing my own socks. Just not clever enough this time.

The movie screen lit up, and I pretended to pay attention to the safety instructions I knew by heart. Respectfully, I turned to see where the nearest emergency exit was for me, located one fifteen rows back, not noticing the one directly to my left until we landed.

Then they ran a clip of the movie they'd be showing, and I brightened when I saw it was something I had drooled through the first time and would be happy to drool through again.

I got out my journal to take my mind off the fact that I was cold, hungry, and bored and no one cared, handily forgetting the fact that my current state was my own fault. I knew about the big picture traveling. I'd backpacked all over Europe. I was a seasoned traveler. What had happened?

I'd gotten lazy.

I'd forgotten to remember my traveling wisdom, so I got out my journal and began making myself a new list.

THINGS TO TAKE TRAVELING:

1. money
2. a sweater or jacket
3. water bottle
4. lip balm
5. mints or gum
6. snacks
7. a book
8. socks

After about an hour, I added "9. pain reliever" because though I seldom had headaches, I had one now and it'd been an hour since I'd asked the nice air hostess for something. Reading over my list, I wished I could think of a tenth item so it'd be easy to count them on my fingers before my next trip.

Well, thank heavens I'm a fast learner because the next time I had to fly, I sat down, kicked off my shoes, pulled on my bunchy socks, unbuttoned my sweater, had a sip of water, put on some lip balm, handed Frédéric his gourmet chicken sandwich I'd made at home, took a bite of my own, and began reading my book before the plane even took off. I felt as chic as a model in the *SELF* magazine I also had and thought about sending them my traveling list as an article proposal.

Then suddenly, I started to panic.

"AH-FOO!" I sneezed through my fingers, spraying chicken sandwich and green grapes in a small radius, including my silk pants and across Frédéric's left arm. He looked at me like he wanted to move over one seat but rolled his eyes instead. I shrugged my shoulders sheepishly.

Tissues, I added mentally to my list of things of traveling wisdom. Never again did I want to be all dressed up with nowhere to sneeze.

Then I smiled. That made ten.

Remember your traveling wisdom.

LIFE SKILL

#9. Taking One Step at a Time

Builds Productivity

65.

A Remote for Kids

"BATMAN," SAID A SMALL CHILD BEHIND US IN THE movie theater. Iain and I smiled in the dark.

Kids.

"Batman," he chimed again, causing us to miss some dialogue. I discreetly turned around and saw a mother sitting with several small children. The news anchor was the one on her lap. He looked about three. Being a big sister, I knew about little people. I had "shhed" my little brother's questions, but whispered the answers in their ears if it was a time when we needed to use our quiet voices.

"Batman!" the little boy sang out, and Iain sighed. This was getting annoying because the kid's volume had increased and we were waiting for the mom to say something like, "Shh, sweetie," but no guidance came.

Perhaps his parents had never said, "Keep it down, guys," like ours had in public places where others might be bothered by our playful noise. In a park, on a playground, or down in the woods, Mom and Dad didn't mind our outside voices as we galloped around.

But if we were out in public and getting a little loud, they'd step in, saying, "Guys, you can talk, but quietly, please." If we wanted to show them something at the museum, for example, we had to walk over to get them, not yell across the exhibition hall, "Hey, Mom, look at this woolly mammoth!"

Why?

"Because people have come for reasons other than to hear you," Dad reminded us.

"BATMAN! BATMAN!" the child yelled louder, and why shouldn't he? His mom hadn't told him to do otherwise. He was excited seeing his caped hero larger than life on the big screen. Heck, we were excited.

I patted Iain's arm and whispered, "Try to enjoy the movie," adding, "too bad they don't make remotes for kids," miming pushing a mute button.

"BATMAN! BATMAN! BATMAN!" the little boy yelled joyfully at the top of his voice, and realizing that sitting there being annoyed wasn't being very productive, I decided to take a different step. I turned around, and looking directly at the little boy with a sincere smile, put my finger over my closed mouth, and *winked* conspiratorially.

And bless his heart, that little guy put his finger over *his* mouth, and was quiet for most of the rest of the movie. He knew how to be quiet, he just didn't know this was a moment to be. Amazing what a little nudge in the right direction can do. He got it in a heartbeat.

Kids.

Be considerate in public.

66.

Picked by Me

PLOP.

I had just picked my first summer strawberry.

Mom had said to go to a part of the field where no one had picked yet, so off I went and plunked my empty cardboard box down on the ground. Right next to Iain's.

"Just kidding," I said, grinning, and hopped over a row.

This is going to be a long day, I thought, kneeling down with a heavy heart, imagining the eternal arc of time from this present moment and my berryless box to the moment when I'd have picked several boxes, as deep as a shoebox and as large as a breakfast tray, and be climbing back into the van to go home. But then I saw a bright red patch of color behind some dark green leaves, and I couldn't help feeling a tiny thrill. To my twelve-year-old eyes, strawberries were like little surprises waiting to be found.

I thought about what Mom had said on the ride over—way too cheerfully—that if we were willing to just begin, one thing would lead to another and pretty soon, we wouldn't even know what our hands were doing. I wasn't too sure, but then, I didn't have much choice. Today was strawberry picking day for making jam.

Oh, joy.

Thus, berry by berry, my box began to turn red, even though I had a few false starts, eating every other one. Then Iain whistled and I turned around and saw that he was in the same place in his row just behind me, and the race was on. We picked fast, but not so fast you plucked off a whole stem with only one red berry but three pink or white ones, which now would never turn red, which I always regretted.

Iain and I tied, and showing Mom our first full boxes, she was full of compliments, saying, "Oh, you guys are so fast," which I now see was so sneaky, so we'd continue picking with happy hearts. Clever.

I filled my second box even faster, partly because I had the hang of it again, and also because I was eating less. Then Iain followed me back to my part of the patch, saying, "Thought you might want some company," and before long, we were lost in conversation, oblivious to what our hands were doing, just as Mom had predicted. What I'd give to know what we talked about that morning, me at twelve and Iain, fifteen.

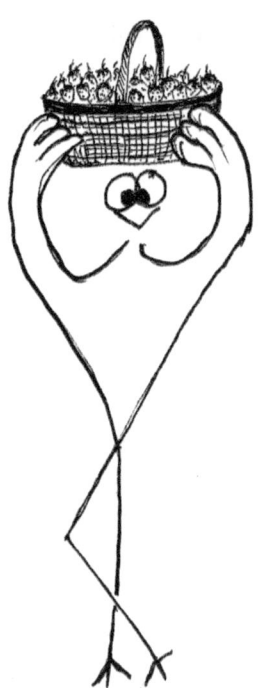

At some point, filling my third box, I invented a new method by filling my T-shirt, then waddling back to my box when it couldn't hold one more berry. And what did I see when I stood up? Iain stealthily stealing berries from my box!

"Stop, thief!" I yelled, as he took off laughing, leaping over the rows toward Mom.

Of course, Iain came back to pick by my side again, bringing us each a fourth empty box to fill, and then Bruce, six, and Douglas, four, came moseying down the row to show us the berries they'd picked. Douglas had a handful of berries rolling around in his box and a stained mouth to prove he'd picked more. Bruce had managed to cover the whole bottom of his box, so what did Iain do? He poured some of his berries into Bruce's box so it was more full. Seeing this, I poured some of my berries into Douglas's and off they went to show Mom.

Another hour later Mom said, "Finish whatever box you're on, and let's go," and I swear the last box filled itself. I suppose it's not because tortoises really are faster than hares, but because when you do find the flow of things, you're not thinking about time anymore. And if you just keep at it, the moment finally comes when whatever you were doing, is now...done.

As the friendly farmer weighed the boxes of strawberries on the scale for the bill, Mom offered to have him weigh Bruce and Douglas too. He just laughed and told us that he hoped we'd all come again next year, too, which we did.

As we drove down the dusty road, an entourage of cars crowded with families was just arriving. How smart I suddenly thought Mom had been to have gotten us up with the sunrise to start picking before the day was hot. It also meant that we were the first ones discovering the berries that the night before in the moonlight weren't ripe yet, but in the pink dawn were. That afternoon after lunch and a nap, it was all hands on deck.

I remember the scene still...Iain, Christopher, and I nipping the green tops off the strawberries with paring knives...Bruce and Douglas standing on chairs to see over the counter in aprons helping Dad measure sugar...Mom cooking the strawberries on the stove...the scent wafting over to us outside. How pretty the bright red jam looked in glass jars lined up on the counter at the end of the day lit from behind with sunshine.

Each jar was opened with tremendous appreciation for all the work that had gone into it, especially during the long winter, and with a bit of rationing, the batch lasted an entire year. And sometimes, a whole berry would land on my piece of toast—*plop*—and I'd wonder if, by chance, it had been picked by me.

Make homemade jam.

67.

What's in a Name?

IT WAS NEARLY TEN AT NIGHT AND I WAS YAWNING and nearly cross-eyed from ironing name tags into the clothes that I'd be taking to summer camp the next morning. But it was the least I could do since Mom had gone back to the store, three miles down our country road late at night, to buy mosquito repellent she thought we had but didn't. She said I'd need a gallon of it. Probably the travel size in Maine, which was where I was going. But when she came back, she didn't look nearly as tired as when she'd left. In fact, she positively sashayed into the living room and handed me a bag.

"I couldn't help it," she said, and I pulled out a hot pink terrycloth bathrobe. "I just imagined you slipping it on coming out of the lake and being cozy. Peek in the pocket," she said, pointing, and I pulled out a hot pink flashlight that fit perfectly into the palm of my fourteen-year-old hand. "See how they match?"

"I love them," I said, loving them. I'd seen these items under the word "optional" at the end of the packing list, but I hadn't said anything because I knew it was already a financial stretch for Mom and Dad to be sending me to summer camp.

"There's something else," she said, shrugging her shoulders helplessly, "so Merry Christmas." It was July. I reached around in what I thought was an empty plastic bag and pulled out a small Swiss Army knife from the bottom of the bag. Pink.

"Oh, Mom," I said, hugging her tightly. "It's so cute. I love it."

"Of course, you have to be careful with knives," she warned. "But now you have something if you get lost in the woods and need to cut down a tree, carve a canoe, or scare off a bear."

"Or file a nail," I said, displaying the nail file, which was next to the scissors and a pair of tweezers. It even had a toothpick. I was ready for the wilderness.

"Let's put your name on these things too," said Mom, "so if you happen to get separated, they might have a chance of getting back to you. But please try to come home with everything," she added, which I managed to do, and which later, Mom said, was the best way of thanking her for my summer experience, along with the letters I wrote home.

Now, as an adult, occasionally Mom still asks if I have my name on things, and sometimes I do and sometimes I just roll my eyes because I don't, until this past weekend.

Frédéric and I were at a wedding in France and halfway into the four-hour drive back home when I realized that I'd left our brand-new video camera on the table so we could dance. The video cassette within was full of special moments, the last one being us moving into our first flat together after we were married. How ironic that I'd planned to mail the cassette to Mom and Dad the day before, but Dad had said, "Make a copy first, just in case," but I hadn't yet.

"Why didn't I put our name on it?" I moaned, thinking back to the night of ironing on my name tags and scratching my name onto my new pink flashlight with my new pink knife.

"I thought you had," said Frédéric, shaking his head.

We called the venue the moment we got home, but no video camera had been turned in. I hardly slept that night, thinking about all the things I had recorded that we could never repeat. Awake in the dark, I promised myself to begin again to put contact information on things that I cared about. Taking that one extra step would inevitably save many unnecessary steps in the future.

As luck would have it, two days later the bride's aunt called us, saying she'd found a lone camera at the end of the evening and taken it home for safe keeping. Then she watched the video and recognized Frédéric, not seeing me since I was the one videoing—including while being carried across the threshold.

Ironically, years later, I found a lone camera sitting on a bench in Venice and took it home for safekeeping. The video turned out to be a wedding, taken by the bride's father no less. But how could I possibly find them? Then the band's name appeared for one fleeting moment and contacting them, they contacted the family, and I made arrangements to meet the father in London where I needed to travel a month later.

"Merry Christmas," I said, handing him the camera. It was March. With shining eyes, he thanked me profusely, and we laughed when he realized that in his haste to meet me, he'd again forgotten something on a bench in the bus. Thank-you flowers.

Put contact information on important items.

68.

Changing a Tire without Superman

"WANNA LEARN HOW TO CHANGE A TIRE?" IAIN ASKED one summer afternoon when I was newly sixteen.

"Why?" I asked suspiciously. "Is there one that's flat?"

"Thankfully, no," he said. "I'm just changing the oil in my car, but it occurred to me that you might get a flat one day, and I'm more fun than your car manual." Imagining myself alone in the middle of nowhere with a flat was all it took.

"You're on," I said and followed him out to the driveway. "So what do we do first?"

"First, we get the little bag of tools inside the spare tire," he said, and I looked at him blankly. He pointed a greasy finger to the back of the car.

So that's where the spare tire is, I thought, finding it hidden beneath the floor of the trunk. *Always wondered about that.*

"Now," he said, pulling out a metal contraption and holding it up, "this is called a thingy-ma-jig. It's how you can change a tire without Superman. It's what lifts up your car."

"That little thing?" I asked, intrigued.

"Yep," he said, pulling over a foam pad and kneeling in front of the back right tire. "First, you position it under the car, right in front of the wheel so it's stable. See that?" he asked. I did. "That way the car won't fall on you. We wouldn't want that to happen, would we?" he added. I gazed down at the top of my brother's head. He was such a carbon copy of Dad, and like Dad—who talked a bit like Yoda—he liked to explain the why behind things. "Then we—wait a minute," he said, moving over to make room for me, "you do it. Then the steps will be in your muscles, since they're already in mine." I knelt down beside him.

"Now," he said, pointing, "take this handle and hook it onto this notch, and we get something called leverage. Leverage is how you can lift a car, your neighbor's car, or any elephant that won't get off the road. You pump it like this," he said, and he started pumping with only one hand. "Or," he said, standing up, "you can step on it." I tried pumping both ways, amazed as the wheel of the car began lifting off the ground.

"Now, we—oops," Iain said, "we forgot something. We have to let the car back down. This is a trick Dad showed me," he said, and we let the car back down. "You loosen the nuts that hold on the tire *before* you raise the car off the ground. That way you have resistance. Otherwise, once the tire's off the ground hanging in midair, loosening the nuts is more difficult." I didn't understand a thing he said until we did just as he explained, and then it made total sense. Now I knew Dad's trick too.

I learned how to chip off the hub cap, loosen the nuts, and even step on the wrench with my weight to loosen the last one, but carefully, not to break the wrench. Then I lifted the tire off—surprisingly heavy—then put it right back on, since it wasn't really flat. Then we reversed the whole process, and holy cow, it wasn't complicated at all one step at a time.

"Et voilà!" Iain said, standing up. "You just changed a tire."

The last thing he showed me was how to check the tire's air pressure, which amused me because I'd always wondered what that thing in the glove compartment was that looked like a thermometer for tires. Now I knew.

Still, I'm grateful that my dear little secondhand car with over 150,000 miles on it has never had a flat tire. I'm also lucky, it turns out, because the last time I took it to a garage to get snow tires put on for my first Vermont winter driving, I'd never have been able to unloosen any of the nuts myself. The mechanic explained that they must've been tightened with an electric drill, which is what he had to use to undo them.

"Pardon me," I said politely, as he was about to retighten the bolts with his drill. "I'd prefer to tighten them myself by hand. You never know when I might get a flat all alone in the middle of nowhere and have to change a tire without Superman."

The car mechanic grinned, handed me his wrench, and said, "You're on."

Know how to change a car tire.

69.

What's behind Door #3?

"SWEETIE, COULD YOU HANDLE THE KITCHEN, PLEASE?" asked Mom as she headed back down the stairs. Seven tiny words and my afternoon was doomed.

I knew it wasn't a question. She and Dad were busy in the studio, Christopher was editing a soundtrack, Iain was mowing around the fruit trees with the hand mower, and Bruce and Douglas, still small, were napping. That left me.

And the kitchen was a wreck.

Time to be a contestant on TV's *The Price Is Right*.

Iain and I had invented our own game when there was a greasy kitchen to clean, knowing it was easier to finish something if you'd just begin.

We'd set the stove timer for five minutes and race each other cleaning a counter. When the buzzer went off, you froze. If you finished before the buzzer, you got a head start on your next counter. If not, you had to finish the first one before moving to the next.

Being alone today, it was me against the clock. And my lively studio audience.

I set the timer and I was off.

I ran to my first counter, boxed up leftovers, rinsed sticky plates, threw out watermelon rinds, and ate the ends of two pickles and some stray potato chips.

Ding! went the first timer.

I raced to the next counter, unloaded the dishwasher with one hand, and loaded dirty dishes with the other.

Ding! went the second alarm, and some audience members applauded.

On the third counter, I filled greasy pots and pans with hot soapy water and began scrubbing. Before I knew it, *Ding!* went the third five minutes.

With only minutes left on the last ticking clock, I dried the pots, put them away, and began scouring the sticky stove. Suddenly, Bob Barker—the illustrious gameshow host—appeared onstage amid thunderous applause.

"Ten, nine, eight," he began counting into his mic, the studio audience joining in.

I rinsed the stove surface and added soap to the dishwasher.

"Five, four, three," Bob continued, the audience chanting louder. I put the broom away at a sprint, turning the dishwasher on as I flew past, and threw my sponge across the kitchen; it landed neatly in the sink.

"Done!" I yelled, raising both hands in the air.

"Two, one," yelled Bob. *Ding!* went the last alarm, and the audience exploded.

"You beat the clock!" cried Bob over the cheering. "What time is it? Time to pick your door!"

"Pick door number one! No, door number two. Pick door number three!" shouted the audience all at once.

"What amazing prizes lie hidden behind?" Bob asked the crowd. "A new washing machine? A trip to Hawaii? A new car?"

Please don't pick the cow, I thought nervously.

The studio atmosphere sizzled with excitement.

"Door number two," I said into my wooden spoon mic. "No wait, door number one," I added hastily. "No, not door number one. Door number three. Door number three!" I repeated with finality.

"What's behiiiiiind door number *three*?" Bob yelled, and I heard the door being slid open. *"It's a brand-new car!"* he thundered, and the crowd went wild.

"Oh, what a beautiful job, honey, thank you," said Mom, appearing behind the door she'd just slid open. "You can be proud."

"I am," I said smugly, tucking the wooden spoon back into the drawer and stepping off the kitchen stage. "I picked the car. Not the cow."

Seven words and my afternoon was saved.

Begin things in order to finish.

70.

Do I Really Need it?

"WHAT DO YOU MEAN IT'S NOT RETURNABLE?" I ASKED the saleswoman incredulously. "This is America. Everything's returnable." But she just nodded in that infuriatingly polite way they nod to problem customers. Then she pointed to the sign above her head: "No refunds, exchanges only."

Huh. Hadn't seen that.

"Well, may I exchange it, then?" I asked.

"Of course," she said politely.

"For cash?" I asked brightly. She shook her head with an "I'm so sorry" smile. She could afford to. She had my money.

"Perhaps I can help you find something you'll be happier with," she said, coming out from behind the counter.

"I'd be happier if you'd credit my charge card," I whispered under my breath. What had I done? I had just spent my entire food allowance for the month. On a shirt.

I'd gone for a walk down Broadway as a study break from exams, when I'd seen a beautiful sleeveless shirt with a single button at the neck so the shirt fell completely open, looking like something a model would wear on a fashion magazine cover. It wasn't until I was home and tried it on in front of the mirror that whatever neurons had been misfiring finally subsided.

"What is wrong with you?" asked the girl in the mirror, aghast. "It's lime green. We don't wear lime green. And have you seen what it's made of?" The price tag said pure silk. I checked anyway. One hundred percent not silk.

"We sweat in polyester, remember?" she reminded me. "What happened to pausing *while* we shop?" she continued. "We've practiced this so, gee, you don't keep buying things you don't need, don't wear, and can't afford. Plus it's so unproductive because then you have to return it, which is a terrible waste of time. More importantly, it's terrible for the environment because most of it's going to end up in a landfill or worse. The ocean is worse. And fish don't need any more lime green shirts."

I hung my head.

"What happened to asking our five questions *before* you buy something? Is it the right color? Size? Material? Price? Do you really, really, *really* need it?" Unfortunately, I didn't, which was why I was back at the store twenty minutes later to exchange it for something I could live with. While I wasn't eating for the month.

I felt hungry already.

"How about this?" asked the nice saleswoman, handing me a watery gray halter top made out of something that felt like plastic.

"Um," I said, trying to sound appreciative, "would you have anything perhaps in natural fibers? Cream? Silky? Soft? Flowing?"

"I'll be right back," she said patiently, and looking at my reflection again, I made a promise to my higher self to one, ask a store's return policy before making a purchase, and two, begin to practice needing *less*.

Again.

Like I used to.

Like Mom had taught me.

No sooner had I made my promise, when over the dressing room door came an ivory silk blouse with a deep V-neck, delicate mother-of-pearl buttons, and long slits on either side that opened as I walked. It was absolutely beautiful. I held my breath and looked at the price tag. It was even seventeen dollars less, which she kindly offered to refund in cash completely against the rules.

I'd eat for two more days.

"We just got it in," the saleslady said through the door. "It's the only one in the whole store."

"It's perfect," I said gratefully. "I'll take it."

I was pretty hungry that month learning a lesson I thought I already knew. I was also ridiculously careful wearing my new silk shirt, pretending I was a cover model as I ate cereal for the month. Still, I'm back on track being a more responsible consumer by lending and borrowing when I can, shopping vintage, selling stuff or giving it away if it's still good but I don't wear anymore, and practicing my fifth rule of thumb. Do I really, really need something new? Probably not. Because when it comes to sustainability, less really is more.

Be a responsible consumer.

71.

A Banana Peel

OH, LOVELY. YEAH, THIS IS REALLY FUN. I SHOULD DO this more often, I thought, looking at the black banana peel I'd just pulled out from under the passenger seat of my car.

I knew this said something about me.

The condition of my car perhaps even reflected what I cared about. I still didn't want to do it.

It was a sunny Saturday, and the last thing I wanted to be doing was vacuuming out my car, especially since I couldn't remember the last time I'd cleaned it. But earlier Mom had needed to borrow my car and embarrassed, I handed over the keys. When she returned home, I was already hooking up the small vacuum cleaner with a mile of extension cord to reach the driveway to avoid any sarcasm about how nice it had been to drive such a clean car.

I opened all four doors and began pulling out anything I couldn't suck up—a half-eaten bag of chips, a single tennis shoe, a library book—oops—some old sunglasses, and well, for heaven's sakes, there's Dad's missing pen.

Then I took out the floor mats and began vacuuming on the

driver's side, and *pling!* something metallic went up the vacuum hose. Probably a penny. I felt underneath the seat, hopeful for more money. Felt some crumpled paper. A ten? Twenty? Nope. A candy bar wrapper.

Then I started vacuuming around the foot pedals and found another penny. A shiny new one. I slipped it in my pocket for good luck and kept on vacuuming.

Then I hauled the vacuum cleaner around to the passenger side, lifted out the floor mats, and found another penny. I put it into my pocket, as well. Then I reached under the passenger seat and felt something…squishy. I froze. But then, since nothing bit me, so whatever it was, was probably dead, I pulled out…the banana peel.

With a penny stuck to it.

That made four, if you counted the one I vacuumed up.

No way! *Douglas.*

I ran back to the house, and there was Douglas waiting for me just outside the kitchen door. "I was wondering how long it'd take you," he said, grinning mischievously.

I'd read a book in school called *Cheaper by the Dozen* about a family with twelve children. One story was about the kids doing chores, but none liked to dust. So on dusting day, the mother hid ten pennies around the house that they would find if they did a thorough job, which they could then keep for candy.

Years later, Douglas complained about his Saturday job of vacuuming one day, so I hid ten pennies around the house and told him that if he found them all, I'd have a little surprise for him at the end.

It became our tradition, just his and mine.

So here Douglas had heard me complaining about having to vacuum on this beautiful Saturday, and he had snooked out to my car and hidden ten pennies. So cute.

"What do I get if I find all ten?" I asked, as we walked back to the car together.

"Oh, that's a surprise," he said, climbing into the car to keep me company. "First, you have to find all ten," he said, which I knew would be tricky because I always hid the last pennies really well.

"But I already sucked one up," I protested, starting up the vacuum cleaner again.

"The one under the banana peel?" he asked, and this time it wasn't just the vacuum cleaner that was howling.

Keep your car clean.

72.

Over the Edge

MY KNEES WERE SHAKING.

My mouth was dry.

My hands were sweaty, but no way was I letting go of the rope that was tied around my waist. It was literally my lifeline.

I smiled bravely for the camera, pretending I didn't feel like I was about to see my breakfast again.

And stepped over the edge.

Into thin air.

I took one shaking, quaking step at a time backward down a sheer rock cliff doing my first rappel. I was held in place by only one other group member, a giant boulder, some nylon rope, and a leader—who I hoped wasn't just looking on as he did sometimes when teaching.

So this is what it feels like to be outside my comfort zone, I thought, my heart pounding. I stared straight ahead, unwilling to look left or right, afraid I'd catch a glimpse of...down. Of course, I was missing the spectacular view on either side being the chicken that I was, creeping down the rockface one inch at a time. I wasn't even brave enough to push off with both feet, let through some rope, and fall a bit through the air.

Breathe, I reminded myself, finding I was holding my breath. *It's one step at a time.*

Chicken, my higher voice helpfully chimed in. *Mountain goats do it better. And they aren't on belay.*

At seventeen, I was the youngest in our group of fifteen people learning skills to explore the wilderness in the Southern Rockies of Wyoming with the National Outdoor Leadership School (NOLS). For five weeks we hiked up to twelve hours a day, carrying thirty-pound backpacks that contained two-person tents, our sleeping bag, cooking equipment, and clothes for any and all weather. Additionally, we each carried a fifteen-pound food bag, replenished every nine days by mules at a designated location.

The packs towered so high over our heads, you only saw your neighbor's legs peeking out from underneath as you walked behind each other along trails made mostly by elk.

In addition to mountain climbing skills and sitting on summits, we had classes on map reading, the stars, rappelling, wilderness survival techniques, and the surrounding flora and fauna, including which plants you could eat in a bind. Who knew that bluebells really do taste like green beans? In a pinch. The experience was both unforgettably wonderful and the hardest thing I'd ever done.

There were moments when I thought I couldn't lift my pack one more time, negotiate through one more boulder field, slide down one more shale trail, climb over one more fallen tree, or scale one more summit.

Once, I was designated to hike last in line and suddenly, the young woman who was hiking in front of me just stopped and I almost bumped into her. So much for security distance.

"I can't take one more step," she said simply, slipping off her backpack and leaving it in the middle of the path. Then she climbed a nearby boulder and lay backward, looking up at the sky. I watched the rest of our group hike up the mountain trail, go around the bend, and disappear from sight. And because it was my job to bring up the rear, I took my backpack off, too, and climbed up onto the boulder next to her, and she sat up.

And there we sat in silence.

"You go on," she finally said with a deep sigh. "You don't have to stay with me. I'm just gonna to stay here for...forever." And I sat there racking my brain trying to think of something uplifting to say.

"Forever's a long time," I finally said helpfully.

"No, I mean it," she answered, her voice breaking. "I can't take one more step. I'm staying here." And she closed her eyes and lay back down.

And little by little, I found myself listening to the wind in the leaves...and the buzzing of tiny things with invisible wings zipping by...and different birds calling...and it was...lovely.

Just sitting there on the boulder.

Waiting.

Then a moment later, my companion sat up and said, "OK, I'm ready to go now," and she hopped off the boulder, strapped on her pack, and off we went up the trail.

Why I suddenly remembered this moment in a single flash, I'll never know but, suddenly, I didn't want to wait for forever and miss this view of a lifetime, even if I was terrified hanging by a single rope over a cliff. And so I peeked to my right and saw... *the entire range of the Rockies.*

"Oh my God," I said, having never seen something from this perspective before. Then I looked to my left, and saw the *rest* of the Rockies continuing out to what looked like Norway. And the magnificence of the view gave me such courage, that though still wildly afraid, I pushed off with both feet, let out some rope, and fell a bit through the air. Probably a whole...two feet. *What a thrill.* Then I did another jump. And a slightly bigger jump after that. That's what stepping out of your comfort zone, even for a little moment, can do. *Change* you.

A little bit or maybe astoundingly.

Either way, you get a new perspective to carry forward from that moment on.

For forever.

Experience things outside your comfort zone.

LIFE SKILL

#10. Being Positive

Builds Joy

73.

A Happy Bed

"MOM, WHY DO I HAVE TO MAKE MY BED?" I called out, seeing Mom pass by my bedroom door in the hallway. I was around nine.

"Because I'm not going to make it for you," she answered, backing up to my doorway.

"No, really," I said.

"No, really," she answered, without missing a beat.

"But I'm just going to get back into it tonight and the rest of my room's all tidy," I said. I stood aside and waved my hand around to show her.

"It's just what we do," she added, turning to leave.

"You always say that," I pressed, and Mom sighed and shifted the laundry basket she was carrying to her other hip.

"Well, for one thing," she offered, considering for a brief moment, "your room reflects you. It demonstrates if you're careful with things or careless. When things are organized, it's easier to have more organized thoughts too. That includes your bed. How's that?"

"Plus, when you make it, you have a happy bed," added Dad, passing by out of the blue.

"A happy bed?" I echoed. "Why didn't you just say so?" And I turned right around and started making it, because at age nine, that made the most sense of all.

Really.

※

Make your bed daily.

74.

The Motorcycle and the Wind

KIDS AREN'T DUMB.

They know if you want to be with them or not.

It doesn't have to be for hours and hours, it just needs to be real, because you never know what moment together may become a memory they will remember for the rest of their lives.

Like the time Dad invited me for a motorcycle ride.

I was four.

We were living in upstate New York, and Dad was sitting on his silver-blue motorcycle. The motor was already running and while he was putting on his helmet, he asked if I wanted a ride as I came down the front steps. He must not have seen that I was barefoot, and when he lifted me off the ground, the top of my left foot accidentally brushed the top of the exhaust pipe, and I got a small burn.

I remember Dad hurrying with me in his arms to the bathroom, sitting me upon the counter, and putting a glob of white cream on the top of my foot. Then he put a small gauze bandage over it and carefully slipped on my tennis shoe, loosening the laces so the flap stayed open.

Then he did something unexpected.

Dad offered me a motorcycle ride anyway.

He could've so easily decided after the little trauma not to. But he did. And it's why I have the memory perfectly in place.

So, you never know the next time you invite someone to do something, if that will become a memory they'll treasure for a lifetime. As in the rest of their lives.

You never know.

You can only be sure that if you don't, they won't, because there's no memory in place for them to remember.

Which is why when Dad and I went swimming recently in a lake, I happened to show him the nearly invisible mark on the top of my left foot that looks a bit like the moon. Apparently, he never knew I had it, and he apologized again. But I surprised him by saying that this faint mark was something I'd always cherished because it reminded me of a day when thirty-six-year-old Dad and four-year-old me took off zooming on a silver-blue motorcycle in the wind.

Make meaningful memories.

75.

Batman's Birthday

IT WAS MY NINTH BIRTHDAY AND THE THEME WAS *Alice in Wonderland*. We were giant playing cards running around with croquet mallets, the poster sheets of paper that we'd made ourselves with crayons worn hanging from our necks with string. After croquet, we girls trooped over to our neighbor's house; they had invited us to swim in their pool of tears.

Mom decorated the lunch table as a tea party and Iain, age twelve, surprised me by appearing as the Mad Hatter, wearing a glitter-covered cardboard top hat he'd made the night before. I hardly recognized him wearing one of Dad's suit jackets with a bow tie and Mom's white gloves. He carried my birthday cake in the shape of Alice with her apron made from blue and white sugar, and Disney's "Have a Very Merry Un-Birthday" played on my record player.

To be clear, our birthdays were not normally celebrated like this, but each of us kids have a memory of one that was. Christopher had a volcano birthday with a volcano cake. Bruce and Douglas each had *Star Wars* birthdays, the kids running around in homemade Darth Vader masks, with one little girl arriving with her braided hair in coils around her ears like Princess Leia.

Our family's birthdays began with mine in April and ended with Dad's at the end of August, and normally, we celebrated them rather simply with a family dinner outside on the picnic table, a few balloons and paper streamers to make the table look festive. There was always a homemade cake with candles, a few wrapped presents, and a birthday photograph to mark the moment. Also, at some point in the day, Dad would find you and say, "We sure are glad you came to play with us so-and-so many years ago today."

Still, the birthday that I remember most was Iain's eighth birthday, even though I was only five. The theme was Batman.

When it was time to take the eight boys back home after the party festivities of running around the grass in their homemade Batman capes that Mom had sewn on her machine, wearing paper Batman masks Dad had painted himself, who should come bursting out of the garage door on his motorcycle?

Batman!

Iain never once recognized Dad on his familiar blue motorcycle, as Dad had painted batwings on his helmet and wore his own superhero cape flying out behind him as he escorted the boys home in the van Mom drove.

The eight-millimeter film Mom got of the look on Iain's face is priceless, and Iain's only birthday regret that evening before bedtime was that Dad hadn't seen Batman too.

Make birthdays special.

76.

Looks like Chicken Grease

YOU NEVER KNOW WHAT LITTLE MOMENTS SOMEONE may remember and treasure.

One day, Mom picked me up from school, already a nice surprise as it saved me an hour and a half bus ride home. As we pulled out of the parking lot, I casually mentioned that there was a lip gloss that some of the cool girls, of which I was not, had started wearing to basketball games on Friday nights, and gee, I'd love to have some too.

"Where can you buy it?" she asked, taking fourteen-year-old me by surprise, because Mom was not sentimental. Practicality was more important.

"At a drug store just down the road," I said, pointing. "Um, the other direction."

"Well, let's go," she said, turning the car around, surprising me again. We found the drug store and, getting out of the car, I told myself they were probably sold out, because I was way too excited and I didn't want to be disappointed. But, no, they had some in stock and before I knew it, I was holding the tiny glass tube in my hands.

I remember it like yesterday.

I remember being slightly amazed that it was made of glass rather than plastic, with yellow and white daisies painted on the sides, with a red plastic screw-on top. Strawberry-flavored.

As we drove away, I pulled down the sunshade to put some on in the tiny mirror and I remember its smell and how buttery the gloss felt on my lips, like when I eat toast. I'm sure I turned to Mom and asked how I looked and I'm sure she said something nice, but mostly I just remember holding the tiny tube in my hands. All the way home.

The next Friday night, Jenna came home with me from school so we could go to the basketball game together, and Dad made a roast chicken for dinner, which was one of her favorites after his famous meatloaf. Saying goodbye as we left for the game, Dad looked at me a second time.

"What's that on your lips, Miss Pie?" he asked. "Looks like chicken grease."

"Daaad," I said, leaning closer so he could get a better look. "It's lip gloss."

"Lip gloss?" he repeated. "Well, chicken grease'd taste better," he added with a grin.

"And if they made that flavor," Jenna admitted, "I'd choose that one." Which if they did, she would.

That night at the basketball game, one of the cool girls saw me using my lip gloss and asked if she could borrow it. I felt positively honored as I handed it to her.

Thanks Mom, for the little things, I thought to myself, aware of the tiny tube's presence in my pocket during the whole game. A little thing that may have looked like chicken grease, but smelled like strawberries.

Little things can matter.

77.

Magic Hands

POOR GRANNY.

She had just walked in the front door after making a nineteen-hundred-mile drive cross-country. It was a trip my maternal grandparents made once a year from Sun City, Arizona, to us in Columbus, Ohio, and it took them two and a half days by car.

After barely being allowed to kiss Mom and Dad and my brothers hello, or go to the bathroom, I'd take her by the hand, lead her back to my bedroom, open my favorite storybook, lie down on my bed, place her hand on my back for her, and say, "Go."

This meant I was ready for my back massage.

Simply put, Granny had magic hands.

Years later, I felt a wee bit guilty thinking about how demanding it seems I was around age ten, but Mom assured me that Granny giving her granddaughter a massage was one of her happiest joys.

I later learned that exchanging massages was something only the women on my mom's side of our family tree did, after once asking Granny why she was so good at it. She reasoned that because her mother had given them to her and her two sisters, it only seemed natural for her to do the same when she was a mother, with her own two girls.

Thus, giving my tiny back a tiny massage while tucking me in at night, Mom was simply continuing a tender tradition she'd been raised with, although it wasn't until I was around thirteen that it occurred to me, one day, to offer Mom a massage, which began our own little tradition.

Curiously, my paternal grandmother never offered to massage my cute little grand-daughterly back, and when I asked her if she had ever had a massage herself, she sadly shook her head no. Her mother had never offered, so she had never learned to offer either, and I felt sorry for this grandmother.

After nearly two decades exchanging massages with Mom, we each think the other has magic hands, and now I'm convinced that massages add so positively to one's well-being, we should start introducing the practice of them to everyone. Everywhere.

I'm serious.

Imagine if you knew that no matter how long or difficult your day was, there was a wonderful and respectful neck, shoulder, or back massage waiting for you at the end of it. How would that make you feel?

Exactly.

We all need to be thoughtfully touched with warm human hands from time to time.

You may even learn that you have magic hands.

Learn how to massage.

78.

Party for One

VERY OFTEN, I LOVE BEING ALONE.

I enjoy the quiet that can come with solitude and how when I'm being quiet, my thoughts unfold.

When I'm alone, Life has my full attention.

And my higher consciousness expands...

So, despite the fun and companionship that came with being a family of seven, there were times that I'd wander down the hill and off into the woods.

Just me with my own vibrations.

When we moved to Ohio from upstate New York, we worked as a whole family taming a small portion of our new property that was wild with woods. We spent the first summer chainsawing dead trees, pulling down poison ivy, digging up stinging nettle, collecting fallen branches, and raking up leaves.

We laid wood chip paths throughout the natural clearings, where lady slippers and foxglove bloomed on their own in the springtime. Once Mom planted some daffodil and tulip bulbs at the bases of a few trees, until she found a woman cutting them one morning and putting them in her basket. Mom asked the lady if she seriously thought that tulips grew in different-colored bouquets at the bases of a few select trees in the wild. Needless to say, Mom never planted tulips down there again.

In the center of a big clearing was a giant sycamore tree. It had a huge hollow entrance at the bottom that you couldn't help peeking into when you passed by, as it was a perfect place for a woodland creature to call home.

On this magnificent tree, Dad hung a wooden plank swing from a bough so high, you could swing in huge arcs back and forth, but also in full circles. Standing on the seat, I'd swing and sing for hours, and with my eyes closed, it felt like I was flying.

Sometimes I'd play a game and hop from pool to pool of sunshine on the forest floor, chewing on fresh clover or a plant Dad showed me with stems that tasted like black licorice. Other times I'd crouch quietly by the small swamp that was covered in bright green duckweed. I'd watch the turquoise dragonflies hover, or spy on the painted turtles sunning themselves on floating logs next to frogs almost perfectly camouflaged on lily pads. In the small creek that ran along one edge of the woods, there were polliwogs and miniature crayfish to catch, but I always let them go after examining their tiny new legs or baby claws.

I took the habit of wandering off alone to college with me, often leaving campus to follow the river that passed through town and led to a covered bridge. There I'd sit with a book, my journal, or a sketch pad, alone with my thoughts, lasting for as long as the sunshine or my snacks held out.

A little party for one.

Alone...I don't talk.

Being quiet...I remember to listen.

Listening...Life has my full attention.

And as my higher consciousness expands, I often learn something new.

Huh. Which I guess means that I'm not really...alone. *Hmm.*

Enjoy being alone.

79.

Mom at the Met

"YEAH, YEAH, I KNOW THIS STUFF," I SAID, LOOKING, but not stopping, in the Egyptian section of the Metropolitan Museum of Art. But Mom was pausing every few feet, reading nearly every caption on almost every card in every case.

"Honey," she said, waving me back several thousand years, "look how incredibly this mummy has aged." I backed up to stand beside her. "Hope I look that good when I'm that old," Mom added, and I leaned over and kissed her on the cheek in reply. I was so happy having Mom visit me for a weekend in the Big Apple.

We walked arm-in-arm through the familiar hallways, pausing before paintings we admired most, dutifully going down one side then looping back to admire the works on the other wall.

We wandered into the halls with marble statues and stood still yet again, amazed. We gazed in wonder at how one got solid stone to look like flowing fabric, whispering between ourselves what would happen if a sculptor sneezed while carving, just when you were almost finished, and there goes the nose! I suggested that maybe that was why so many statues were missing that part.

That's what started it.

Mom started giggling into my shoulder and hearing her, I started giggling, pantomiming being a sculptor and accidentally chipping off a nose. After that, Mom and I were pretty much goners. The tiniest thing would crack us both up. All I had to do was raise an eyebrow or make some small gesture with my finger in front of an artwork, and both Mom and I were snuffling into our sweaters again. Finally, it got so bad, we had to hold each other up, silently gasping for breath, tears of stifled laughter rolling down our cheeks.

It wasn't always like this between us, but when it was, it was memorable, and this was one of those moments, being at the Met with Mom.

When we were finally composed enough to continue—having made a pact to not even *look* at each other for a few rooms—I went around a corner into a salon of Dutch paintings. There I found myself face-to-face with a work where honey-colored sunshine illuminated a farm with a huge sky filled with golden clouds and tiny windmills in the distance.

I leaned in as far as was respectful in order to examine the incredible detail. The strokes were so small, the paintbrush must have been a toothpick.

How do they do that? I wondered, marveling at a rooster so real I thought he'd peck my nose for peering so closely, even if he was only one inch tall. How differently these patient strokes and patterns were compared to Dad's paintings with his great sweeping marks, mostly in blues and greens. Memories came back to me of being small and wandering through galleries with Dad, who carefully guided our young, impressionable eyes to look at things with an open mind.

He dared us not to be too quick to decide whether we liked a work or not, but to look until we found something interesting about it. "Something moved the artist to create this," Dad reminded us. "That's their gift to us. The chance to be moved." Seeing it that way, I often was.

Nevertheless, realizing our attention spans could be fickle, Mom and Dad zipped us kids through some gallery or museum exhibits as if we were on rollerblades, and other times, we stopped long enough to learn a fact about a dinosaur bone, the age of a fossil, or how much a blue whale weighed—around two hundred tons, four hundred thousand pounds, or thirty-three elephants—hoping to pique our curiosity, so we'd read a caption in the next room too.

Still, I've always had a harder time understanding modern art, especially since my last visit to the MoMA with Christopher, where I found myself standing in front of a piece of twisted chicken wire stapled to a hunk of wood hanging on the wall.

How do you know that's the real work? I thought innocently, looking at it from different angles to see if I was missing something. *Maybe the person installing the exhibition got it wrong and accidentally hung up what the work had been shipped in? Maybe the actual work is lying against a wall in the museum's warehouse somewhere, patiently waiting to be hung?* Could be.

Then we passed a giant white canvas with one red scribbly mark on it. I was polite enough not to whisper, "I could do that," but I still didn't understand why it was interesting enough to be hanging on the wall of the MoMA.

"Good art has a way of asking us to keep looking differently out of our eyes," Christopher offered, reading my mind, though I still wasn't sure what qualities defined good art.

As lunchtime approached, I asked Mom if she wanted to sit down on a bench near the Tiffany stained glass windows, while I went to see what the soup of the day was at the museum café, and she gratefully accepted with a tiny yawn.

A few minutes later, I came back and saw the loveliest still life upon that bench. I sat down next to it so I could admire it more closely, although I knew every line and curve by heart. There was no title card on the wall behind it, but if there had been, it might have read, *Napping Mama Angel*. Mom had fallen asleep.

Mothers. They really are a work of art.

Visit museums and art galleries.

80.

A Magic Carpet Ride

SO UNEXPECTED.

I was going home for the weekend to see Mom and Dad.

Graduate classes got canceled, and I found a cheap flight and was on my way.

So easy.

I had only a backpack, no homework, and no traffic to the airport.

Then in a heartbeat, everything changed.

The word appeared in red.

"Canceled." Right next to my flight number.

Huh.

How fast things can change.

I guess I wasn't going home.

Well, nothing to do but hold the peace and see what step unfolded next.

I walked briskly to the airline counter.

Trying not to run, which felt…panicky.

It was almost the farthest counter away. As usual.

No one else was there. Where was the line?

"There's one seat left on the last flight out to Minneapolis," said the nice lady behind the counter, "if you've no luggage to check."

Nope.

"But you might need to...run," she said, smiling. "They're already boarding. I'll let them know you're coming, but I can't promise. All you can do is try."

My stomach lurched. Because I would try.

I raced to security from my already faraway counter.

Impossible. Too many people.

Then the guy opened up a new line right in front of me.

Suddenly, the last was first, and that was me.

I whizzed through security.

A way suddenly seemed possible.

Nothing to do now but run.

Instantly, my mouth was dry, my heart was thumping, my hands were sweaty, and I was honestly nauseous. But still, I ran.

I can do this. I did track. Doesn't matter it was thirteen years ago.

I ran, dodging people who seemed to be standing still compared to me.

I screeched to a halt only to confirm my gate.

My knees quaking. My legs shaking.

My gate would be the farthest away. Like always.

No matter the city, I'm almost always the farthest away.

Not tonight. Mine was right around the corner.

I careened around the corner and nearly took down a couple walking while holding hands.

"Pardon me! So sorryyyy."

Too late.

The gate was empty.

Only two staff members behind a quiet counter.

No last person walking through the door.

I couldn't speak, supporting myself with my hands on my knees.

"I need you to stand up, dear, so I can see your face," the lady said kindly, looking at my passport. "It's OK," she said. "You made it. Someone called. We knew you were coming."

My knees buckled.

"You got the last seat on the last flight out tonight. Happy you."

It happens like that sometimes.

Mom and I call it a magic carpet ride.

When you unexpectedly find that the path you were on is no longer available to take, but then a different step appears.

Just one.

And in faith, you take it.

And then, a next step unfolds from the one you just took.

And as you move down this new path, it continues unfolding just one step ahead of you.

Until you end up where you wanted to go.

You just arrived a different way.

So unexpected.

I was on my way home for the weekend to see Mom and Dad. What a joy.

Thank you. Just...thank you.

Sometimes a new path appears when you least expect it.

81.

A Blue Egg

(LATE SUMMER, 1996)

It was the hour before sunset and the lake was turning gold. The geese were honking somewhere on a distant shore, the squirrels were playing their last game of tag in the treetops, and the fish were beginning to jump, even though I was never fast enough to see one. I only heard the splashes and saw rings appear, radiating outward upon the water's surface.

Frédéric was walking among the trees, searching for the right-shaped sticks, finding one here, and another one way over there. I was searching along the shoreline, plucking long blades of grass from the water's edge. I came across a single white fluffy feather, a tiny acorn, and a fallen leaf that went from green to yellow to orange to red across its single surface, and brought them all back to Frédéric, who was now sitting cross-legged on the grass trying to weave his small sticks into a nest.

Then the twig he was gently bending snapped in two. "Birds do it better," he said, shaking his head.

"And only with their feet and beaks," I added helpfully. "Let's try weaving the grass together," I suggested, and dividing my bunch into three sections, began showing Frédéric how to braid.

As he wove, I thought about the birds' nests I'd found when I was small, remembering the thrill of climbing a tree, peeking inside the empty nest, and finding a tiny broken blue eggshell that fit on the top of my little finger.

After several tries, Frédéric and I finally had a sweet little nest, almost round, and he tucked in the downy feather, yellow-to-red leaf, and acorn for decoration. Then Dad called us to dinner, and back up at the house, Frédéric placed the nest in the center of the picnic table on the balcony Mom had set for dinner. Then he placed one more thing in the center of the nest. A small wooden sky-blue egg.

Dad got it the moment he sat down.

He looked up at Frédéric and me with the sweetest expression on his face, instantly blinking back tears with a great big smile.

Then Mom sat down and didn't notice a thing.

She passed around the barbecued chicken, the ears of corn, the green beans, and the ripe red tomatoes from the farmers' market down the road. It was a lovely dinner. Finally, Dad brought out dessert, and I couldn't help myself.

"Have you seen the nest?" I asked, looking directly at Mom, trying to sound casual.

"Yes," Mom said, spooning whipped cream onto her strawberry shortcake, "very pretty."

"We *made* it," Frédéric added, grinning.

"Oh?" said Mom, looking at it more carefully. "I thought maybe you found it down by the lake."

"Have you seen what's *in* the nest?" asked Dad, unable to keep quiet any longer.

Mom looked again and suddenly, she got it.

I nodded with a grin, patting my flat tummy.

"Sometime in April," Frédéric said, beaming.

Life willing, I added silently, offering to keep things in Life's hands, and finally, Dad was allowed to cry.

Remember that Life has its own timing.

In an Eggshell

LIFE SKILL: #1. HOLDING THE PEACE...BUILDS CALM

1. Hold the Peace: Stay calm in a crisis to think clearly.
2. Pat-Pat: Offer pats for comfort.
3. All Tucked In: Have a peaceful bedtime routine.
4. Where Would I Be if I Were a Passport?: Know where important documents are.
5. The Flaming Sword: Forgive with grace.
6. Squish, Squish: Arrive and depart with grace.
7. Whoosh!: Beware of rushing.
8. Always the Sky: Being under the open sky can calm.

LIFE SKILL: #2. BELIEVING IN THE PROCESS...BUILDS PATIENCE

9. Thump-Thump: Remember that Life is a process.
10. Potatoes with Pa: Grow a garden.
11. F-r-e-d: Learn to type without looking at your fingers.
12. Not Ready Yet: There's a moment for everything.
13. Par Lay Voo Fran Say?: Learn to speak a foreign language.
14. My Happy List: Remember simple things that make you happy.
15. Brighter in the Morning: Things look brighter in the morning.
16. Every Hundred Years: Flowing works better than forcing.

LIFE SKILL: #3. OFFERING FEELINGS...BUILDS BALANCE

17. Offering Feelings: Offering feelings builds balance.
18. We Don't Bite: Maintain clear behavior boundaries.
19. Fuzzy Teeth: Have healthy personal hygiene.
20. Little Kindnesses: Practice being thoughtful.
21. Knock-Knock: Upset feelings have negative power.
22. Wait Three Days: Wait three days before sharing news.
23. Talking like a Tennis Ball: Speak thoughtfully.
24. Sitting Smaller than Sunflowers: Remember that Life knows our hearts.

LIFE SKILL: #4. LETTING GO...BUILDS FREEDOM

25. Just You 'n' Me: Sometimes make a memory for just two.
26. I Trust Me: Monitor what you watch.
27. Superhero: Celebrate the wisdom of each new year.
28. Wonder Twins: Respect every soul.
29. A Moose on the Dunes: Sometimes be spontaneous.
30. The Runaway Guitar: Choose your feelings.
31. Once Seventeen: Ask elders for their stories.
32. Pink Pauses: Just be kind.

LIFE SKILL: #5. BEING LOVING & RESPECTFUL...BUILDS KINDNESS

33. Toads and Diamonds: Tone speaks louder than words.
34. Carrots Don't Hop: Appreciate someone else's cooking.
35. A Most Gracious Guest: Be a gracious guest.
36. The Midnight Message: Be your most loving self.
37. Magic Hugs: Hugs are filled with magic.
38. Oh, It Was Nothing: Appreciate someone's effort and time.
39. Tucked into Your Pocket: Stay in touch with those you care about.
40. Just in Case You're Starving: Be a gracious host.

LIFE SKILL: #6. LOOKING FOR THE BIG PICTURE...BUILDS UNDERSTANDING

41. Like the Big Dipper: Ponder why you're here.
42. Broccoli for Breakfast: Eat healthily.
43. I'd Rather Vacuum than Floss: Take good care of your teeth.
44. Slouching: Maintain healthy posture.
45. Don't Start: Don't start smoking.
46. Thoughts on Fire: Be curious.
47. Crunchy Air: Eat breakfast daily.
48. Chocolate Melts: Have an emergency car kit.

LIFE SKILL: #7. WATCHING WHICH WAY WE'RE GOING...BUILDS RESPONSIBILITY

49. Being With: Allow others to participate.
50. Not without That Chicken: Be responsible with money.
51. Who's Wearing My Raincoat?: Take care of your things.
52. Who Had Toast?: Tidy up after yourself.
53. Butter on Your Elbow: Practice good manners.
54. Thinking Drinking: Be responsible with alcohol.
55. Mail Plane: Stay organized.
56. Where's the Moose?: Always look behind you.

LIFE SKILL: #8. LISTENING WITHIN...BUILDS WISDOM

57. Cucumbers in Her Purse: Pay attention to your health.
58. Una Siesta: Naps can work wonders.
59. Ah-Choo!: Take extra care when you're sick.
60. Black Ice: Pay attention to inner messages.
61. So Not OK: Be honest about your mental well-being.
62. The Best in Me: Choose a partner who inspires your highest self.
63. Ol' Coot: Exercise for fun and health.
64. All Dressed Up and Nowhere to Sneeze: Remember your traveling wisdom.

LIFE SKILL: #9. TAKING ONE STEP AT A TIME...BUILDS PRODUCTIVITY

65. A Remote for Kids: Be considerate in public.
66. Picked by Me: Make homemade jam.
67. What's in a Name?: Put contact information on important items.
68. Changing a Tire without Superman: Know how to change a car tire.
69. What's behind Door #3?: Begin things in order to finish.
70. Do I Really Need It?: Be a responsible consumer.
71. A Banana Peel: Keep your car clean.
72. Over the Edge: Experience things outside your comfort zone.

LIFE SKILL: #10. BEING POSITIVE…BUILDS JOY

73. A Happy Bed: Make your bed daily.
74. The Motorcycle and the Wind: Make meaningful memories.
75. Batman's Birthday: Make birthdays special.
76. Looks like Chicken Grease: Little things can matter.
77. Magic Hands: Learn how to massage.
78. Party for One: Enjoy being alone.
79. Mom at the Met: Visit museums and art galleries.
80. A Magic Carpet Ride: Sometimes a new path appears when you least expect it.
81. A Blue Egg: Remember that Life has its own timing.

Bye!

www.ingramcontent.com/pod-product-compliance
Lightning Source LLC
Chambersburg PA
CBHW060513080526
44586CB00012B/473